Authors

Matteo Bortolu
Engin Polat

Reviewers

Betim Drenica
Matheus Guimaraes
Paul Leman
Tom Opgenorth
Chris van Wyk

Commissioning Editor

Veena Pagare

Acquisition Editor

Meeta Rajani

Content Development Editor

Deepti Thore

Technical Editor

Vivek Arora

Copy Editor

Safis Editing

Project Coordinator

Shweta H Birwatkar

Proofreader

Safis Editing

Indexer

Aishwarya Gangawane

Graphics

Disha Haria

Production Coordinator

Nilesh Mohite

About the Authors

Matteo Bortolu currently works in Singapore for Sixscape Communication as Lead Mobile Developer.

He grew up with a strong passion for IT and right after his master of science degree in 2006, the software industry transformed his biggest talent and passion into an enthusiastic software developer.

After more than 20,000 hours of writing backend and frontend solutions based on Microsoft technologies, he met Xamarin in 2012 and felt in love with it.

He has played key roles in mobile projects for worldwide customers, deploying to the stores a wide category of apps such as games, health industry apps, messaging apps, energy industry apps, virtual reality apps, and others.

When he is not in front of a laptop he loves reading, playing the saxophone, and exploring this planet. He loves to share his experiences on his blog (`http://bortolu.com`).

Back in 2014 he founded the Xamarin Developers Facebook group (`https://www.facebook.com/groups/xamarin.developers`), which currently has more than 14,000 members.

Xamarin 4 By Example

Design, develop, and publish your own mobile apps for iOS and Android using C# and Xamarin Studio

Matteo Bortolu

Engin Polat

BIRMINGHAM - MUMBAI

Xamarin 4 By Example

First published: August 2016

Production reference: 1250816

Published by Packt Publishing Ltd.

Livery Place

35 Livery Street

Birmingham B3 2PB, UK.

ISBN 978-1-78528-290-4

www.packtpub.com

Engin Polat has been involved in many large-and medium-scale projects on .NET technologies as a developer, architect, and consultant and has won many awards since 1999.

Since 2008, he has given training to many large enterprises in Turkey about Windows development, web development, distributed application development, software architecture, mobile development, cloud development, and more.

Apart from this, he organizes seminars and events in many universities in Turkey about .NET technologies, Windows platform development, cloud development, web development, and game development.

He shares his experiences on his personal blog (http://www.enginpolat.com). He has MCP, MCAD, MCSD, MCDBA, and MCT certifications. Since 2012 he has been recognized as a Windows Platform Development MVP (Most Valuable Professional) by Microsoft. Between 2013 and 2015, he was recognized as a Nokia Developer Champion; very few people in the world are given this award. Since 2015 he has been recognized as a Regional Director by Microsoft.

He has also reviewed *Mastering Cross-Platform Development with Xamarin* and *Xamarin Blueprints*.

I'd like to thank my dear wife, Yeliz, and my beautiful daughter, Melis Ada, for all the support they gave me while I was working on this book project.

About the Reviewers

Matheus Guimaraes is the founder and CEO of Guimak Ltd. He's been in the industry since 2002 and served as CTO, principal architect, and technical consultant for various companies over the years. He's been involved in many projects, including The Daily Mail, Xbox, Moonpig, Tesco, and PRS for Music. His latest passion is developing games with Unity and mobile apps with Xamarin. He is a certified Xamarin developer, and his company has been a Xamarin consulting partner since 2015.

Chris van Wyk is a Xamarin University trainer with 18 years of experience in the IT industry. In his various roles as developer, team lead, architect, and software development manager, Chris has been involved in both backend and frontend software development and delivery. With the initial releases of MonoTouch and MonoDroid in 2010, now Xamarin, the development story of mobile was too enticing not to explore. Chris believes Xamarin is the perfect development platform for developers to create applications that delight users across mobile platforms.

www.PacktPub.com

eBooks, discount offers, and more

Did you know that Packt offers eBook versions of every book published, with PDF and ePub files available? You can upgrade to the eBook version at www.PacktPub.com and as a print book customer, you are entitled to a discount on the eBook copy. Get in touch with us at customercare@packtpub.com for more details.

At www.PacktPub.com, you can also read a collection of free technical articles, sign up for a range of free newsletters and receive exclusive discounts and offers on Packt books and eBooks.

https://www2.packtpub.com/books/subscription/packtlib

Do you need instant solutions to your IT questions? PacktLib is Packt's online digital book library. Here, you can search, access, and read Packt's entire library of books.

Why subscribe?

- Fully searchable across every book published by Packt
- Copy and paste, print, and bookmark content
- On demand and accessible via a web browser

Table of Contents

Preface

Microsoft released .NET Framework in February 2002 for Windows platform. The Mono Project was released in June 2004, and it brought .NET to Linux and Mac OS. In 2 years, the Mono Project creators saw a potential in C# and .NET, but they progressed slowly and in 2011, the Mono Project version 1.1 was released.

The Mono Project evolved in time and transformed into a huge cross-platform framework, changing its name to Xamarin.

In February 2016, Microsoft announced that it had acquired Xamarin, and later it was made free and open source.

At the time of writing, Microsoft is the biggest company investing in cross-platform development and helping developers to build applications easily.

Xamarin has several components that develop, build, and package projects in order to publish them on stores. A few such examples are Xamarin.Android, Xamarin.iOS, and Xamarin.Forms. Xamarin.Android and Xamarin.iOS solutions are targeting individual platforms such as Android and iOS. On the other hand, Xamarin.Forms targets all platforms in one solution.

In this book, you'll learn how to use Xamarin.Forms to develop cross-platform applications with different page types, layouts, views, and design patterns by using them.

What this book covers

Chapter 1, *Getting Started with Xamarin*, will help us discover the basics of cross-platform development and where its latest version Xamarin 4 fits. We'll also learn how to use the latest version, Xamarin Studio 6, as the IDE.

Chapter 2, *Sharing Code between Platforms*, will differentiate between Portable Class Libraries and Shared Projects. We will also explore the fundamentals of the MVVM pattern by using it.

Chapter 3, *Exploring the UI Controls*, will explain all the page types, layout types, view elements, and rendering models provided by the Xamarin framework out of the box.

Chapter 4, *Data – the Monkeys Catalog,* will show how the readers to create base types of entities, data access layers, business layers in order to use them along with any project that we'll develop. We'll also create core implementations of them.

Chapter 5, *Cloud and Async Communication,* will help us explore different formats, data, and channel types when communicating with a remote server. We'll explore the differences between a RESTful service and a WSDL service and develop a sample application.

Chapter 6, *Custom Renderers,* will describe customer renderers by creating one. Also, we'll learn to use AppLinks by example.

Chapter 7, *Monkey Puzzle Game – Processing Images,* will help us develop an example project from scratch. We'll develop custom renderers to complete the project.

Chapter 8, *The People Around Me Application,* explains how to develop an example project from scratch. We'll start preparing our development machine and end with a ready-to-publish application. We'll develop and communicate with a web backend in this example project.

Chapter 9, *Testing – Spot the Bugs,* will explain the importance of debugging, testing, and profiling. We'll learn about the different log panels of Xamarin Studio 6. We'll also learn the fundamentals of Xamarin Profiler and the Xamarin.UITest Framework.

Chapter 10, *Publishing to the Market,* helps us finalize this book by publishing a project to all three stores. Starting from building the project, we'll investigate the steps of creating developer accounts, readying the publish package, and uploading them to the stores.

What you need for this book

You'll need a computer and reliable Internet connection. Here is a full-featured list of the required applications:

- Windows 10 OS or Mac OS X
- Xamarin Studio 6
- Visual Studio 2015 Community Edition
- Android SDK
- Xcode (if you have Mac machine and want to build iOS applications)

Apple requires iOS applications to be compiled on a Mac computer, Xamarin requires as well. All required applications can be downloaded from `http://xamarin.com/download` and `https://www.visualstudio.com` pages.

Who this book is for

This book is great if you're already familiar with C# and want to break down the walls of developing applications to a single platform. It's assumed that you have a good knowledge of the object-oriented programming paradigm.

If you want to be familiar with developing applications to all three platforms (Windows, Android, and iOS), this book is for you.

Conventions

In this book, you will find a number of text styles that distinguish between different kinds of information. Here are some examples of these styles and an explanation of their meaning.

Code words in text, database table names, folder names, filenames, file extensions, pathnames, dummy URLs, user input, and Twitter handles are shown as follows: "We can start creating a folder called `Base` and a folder called `Core` inside the main Xamarin Form project."

A block of code is set as follows:

```
using SQLite.Net.Attributes;

namespace XamarinByExample.MonkeysCatalogue
{
    public class BaseEntity<TKey>
    {
        [PrimaryKey]
        public TKey Key {
            get;
            set;
        }
    }
}
```

New terms and **important words** are shown in bold. Words that you see on the screen, for example, in menus or dialog boxes, appear in the text like this: "To use a WSDL, we need to right-click on the project and select **Add a Web Reference**:"

 Warnings or important notes appear in a box like this.

 Tips and tricks appear like this.

Reader feedback

Feedback from our readers is always welcome. Let us know what you think about this book-what you liked or disliked. Reader feedback is important for us as it helps us develop titles that you will really get the most out of. To send us general feedback, simply e-mail feedback@packtpub.com, and mention the book's title in the subject of your message. If there is a topic that you have expertise in and you are interested in either writing or contributing to a book, see our author guide at www.packtpub.com/authors.

Customer support

Now that you are the proud owner of a Packt book, we have a number of things to help you to get the most from your purchase.

Downloading the example code

You can download the example code files for this book from your account at http://www.packtpub.com. If you purchased this book elsewhere, you can visit http://www.packtpub.com/support and register to have the files e-mailed directly to you.

You can download the code files by following these steps:

1. Log in or register to our website using your e-mail address and password.
2. Hover the mouse pointer on the **SUPPORT** tab at the top.
3. Click on **Code Downloads & Errata**.
4. Enter the name of the book in the **Search** box.
5. Select the book for which you're looking to download the code files.
6. Choose from the drop-down menu where you purchased this book from.
7. Click on **Code Download**.

Once the file is downloaded, please make sure that you unzip or extract the folder using the latest version of:

- WinRAR / 7-Zip for Windows
- Zipeg / iZip / UnRarX for Mac
- 7-Zip / PeaZip for Linux

The code bundle for the book is also hosted on GitHub at `https://github.com/PacktPublishing/Xamarin-4-By-Example`. We also have other code bundles from our rich catalog of books and videos available at `https://github.com/PacktPublishing/`. Check them out!

Errata

Although we have taken every care to ensure the accuracy of our content, mistakes do happen. If you find a mistake in one of our books-maybe a mistake in the text or the code-we would be grateful if you could report this to us. By doing so, you can save other readers from frustration and help us improve subsequent versions of this book. If you find any errata, please report them by visiting `http://www.packtpub.com/submit-errata`, selecting your book, clicking on the **Errata Submission Form** link, and entering the details of your errata. Once your errata are verified, your submission will be accepted and the errata will be uploaded to our website or added to any list of existing errata under the Errata section of that title.

To view the previously submitted errata, go to `https://www.packtpub.com/books/content/support` and enter the name of the book in the search field. The required information will appear under the **Errata** section.

Piracy

Piracy of copyrighted material on the Internet is an ongoing problem across all media. At Packt, we take the protection of our copyright and licenses very seriously. If you come across any illegal copies of our works in any form on the Internet, please provide us with the location address or website name immediately so that we can pursue a remedy.

Please contact us at `copyright@packtpub.com` with a link to the suspected pirated material.

We appreciate your help in protecting our authors and our ability to bring you valuable content.

Questions

If you have a problem with any aspect of this book, you can contact us at `questions@packtpub.com`, and we will do our best to address the problem.

1
Getting Started with Xamarin

Ladies and gentlemen, this is Engin and Matteo and we are your chief flight attendants. On behalf of Xamarin Developers Crew, welcome aboard! This is a non-stop service from C# to multiplatform mobile development. Our flight time will be as long as you prefer. We will be exploring exciting examples, trying to cover all the basic and some advanced topics of mobile development. Now make sure your seat and desktop are in the most comfortable position. At this time, we request that all electronic devices be switched in to developer mode. You will find this and all the other useful information in the book located in front of you. We strongly suggest that you read it before take-off. If you have any questions, don't hesitate to e-mail us. We wish you all an enjoyable flight.

Take off

Before we learn what *cross-platform* is, we will explore the meaning of platform specific native apps.

A native app is an app that uses the native **Software Development Kit (SDK)**, and compiles and runs on one specific platform.

It is usually developed using the default programming language of the SDK.

We can write a native iOS app using Xcode as **Integrated Development Environment (IDE)** and Objective-C/Swift as languages, taking advantage of the iOS SDK.

A native Android app is written using Eclipse or Android Studio as IDE, Java as language, and the Android SDK as development kit.

A native Windows Phone app is written using Visual Studio as IDE, C# as language, and .NET as Framework.

This is the classic way to develop apps and for some developers, it is still the best way.

Platform specific native development gives some advantages. The first is that we can rely on the OS manufacturer publishing stable updates and we can always be one of the first to use them.

Also, apps written with native tools and languages have performance, security and better user experience advantages. Hybrid apps basically mobile focused web apps built with HTML5 and JavaScript, wrapped in a native container. Native languages and tools (compilers, linkers, and so on) generates more platform specific and natural outputs (binaries). More platform specific binaries more performant apps, generally it means speed.

It also has disadvantages, such as:

- We need to know three languages in order to develop the same app for the three platforms
- We cannot share the business logic between different platforms and we need to develop and maintain three different business logics
- The code of one platform is mostly not understandable to those who use the other platform

In big companies, the platform specific approach works because most of them have a lot of people dedicated to a project and probably they can afford three different teams. Each one of the teams usually works independently to develop the same app in each single platform. The iOS team cannot share a single line of code with the Android team nor the Windows Phone team, or vice versa. This is called the Silo approach.

People usually think about cross-platform mobile development as **Write Once, Run Anywhere** (**WORA** approach).

The main advantage of this approach is that we can write something that looks like a WebApp that runs everywhere. There are technologies such as Cordova, Titanium, and others based on WORA. They are all based on the lowest common denominator and can be extendable with plugins to support platform specific features such as NFC or Force Touch, and others.

We generally cannot take full advantage of the features offered by each platform.

Platform-specific features are mostly related to the capabilities of the OS installed and the hardware available in the device. They impact the overall user experience.

From Mono to Xamarin

Mono is an open source implementation of the Microsoft .NET Framework based on the **Common Language Runtime (CLR)**.

It was initially released in 2004 after three years of open source development launched by a small team of people that included the current founder and CEO of Xamarin, Miguel De Icaza.

 Xamarin is derived from Mono framework, which is a cross-platform implementation of .Net Runtime. Xamarin was acquired by Microsoft and open sourced all Xamarin frameworks in February 2016. Microsoft also open sourced .Net Framework and made a cross-platform implementation of it, called .Net Core Framework.

MonoTouch was initially released in 2009 and in 2013 its name became Xamarin.iOS.

Xamarin.iOS is a set of libraries (.dll files) that bind the native iOS SDK.

The iOS binding is the way Xamarin maps the idioms used in Objective-C to the idioms used in .NET.

Mono for Android was initially released in 2011 and in 2013 its name became Xamarin.Android. It is a set of libraries that bind the native Android SDK APIs.

The Android binding maps the idioms used in Java to the idioms used in .NET.

Xamarin.iOS and Xamarin.Android are extendable.

A binding project can be written in order to wrap libraries written in Java or Objective-C into a dll that can be used from our C# projects.

Each single feature of the operating system, third-party libraries, and even our own native libraries can be ported writing a binding project.

The architecture of Xamarin allows us to use the best that iOS SDK can offer to iOS based-devices and the best that Android SDK can offer to Android-based devices.

Xamarin adds another value from the developers' point of view: it allows us to use most of the features of the .NET Framework while developing for Android and iOS devices.

From Xamarin to native

Xamarin.iOS based C# code is compiled using **ahead-of-time** (**AOT**) compilation. The resulting compilation output produces a single statically compiled ARM binary.

AOT compilation pre-generates all the native code that the **Just in Time** (**JIT**) compiler would normally generate from the **Intermediate Language** (**IL**). IL is stripped from the managed assemblies, leaving only metadata. AOT links the metadata together with the JIT-less runtime into a single native binary that can be signed with the Apple account.

 An Apple Developer account is needed in order to publish the application to the App Store for iOS devices.
For more information, visit `https://developer.apple.com`.

The Xamarin.Android application runs within the Mono execution environment (also known as Mono Virtual Machine). The Mono Virtual Machine runs side-by-side with the Dalvik Virtual Machine. Dalvik is an integral part of the Android software stack. It is a process virtual machine in the Android operating system that executes applications written for Android.

The connections between the two virtual machines are created by two **Java Native Interface** (**JNI**) bridges:

- **Android callable wrappers**: These are used any time the Android runtime needs to invoke managed code
- **Managed callable wrappers**: These are used any time the managed code needs to invoke Android code

The managed callable wrappers are generated via `.jar` binding and are responsible for converting between managed and Android types.

Xamarin cross-platform

With Xamarin we have different ways to share code.

In general, we want to create a platform specific app writing the most common code we can.

As we can see in the following image, Xamarin.Forms provides shared app logic and shared UI code across platforms. With that support, we can easily develop one true application running and displaying the same on all the platforms.

But there is a thin layer on top of shared layers, and that thin layer adds platform-specific customizations to the Xamarin.Forms projects:

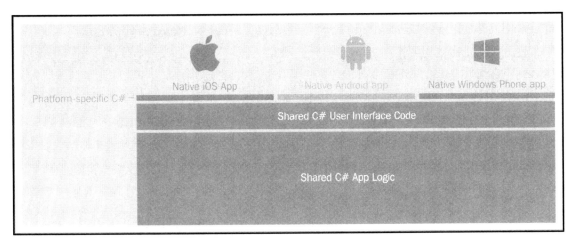

The ways to share the common code are:

- Portable Class Libraries
- Shared Projects

Shared Projects work in a similar way to file linking. All the files contained in a Shared Project are conceptually copied into each referencing project and compiled as part of them.

Portable Class Libraries (PCL) allow us to produce libraries that can be shared across multiple platforms including Xamarin.iOS, Xamarin.Android, and Windows Phone.

When we develop a PCL, we can reference and use it in each platform specific project.

Xamarin.Forms is a UI Toolkit that allows us to share most of the UI components across platforms. Xamarin.Forms has been implemented as a .NET PCL.

What do we need to start?

To develop iOS Apps, we need a Mac in order to compile and run the code.

Xamarin and Microsoft both provide us with very useful and productive IDEs. Microsoft offers a state of the art IDE, Visual Studio, and its free edition Visual Studio Community to us to create cross-platform applications.

Xamarin offers the free Xamarin Studio to us to create cross-platform applications.

Microsoft's Visual Studio runs on Windows, while Xamarin's Xamarin Studio runs on Windows, Linux, and Mac OS.

We also need an App Store account that allows us to download the iOS SDK and Xcode. To develop iOS applications using C#, we need to download and install onto our Mac both Xamarin Studio and Xamarin.iOS.

We will learn more about Xamarin Studio later in this chapter.

To develop Android apps, we need to install the Android SDK.

We can access the Android SDK Manager directly from Xamarin Studio as well as Visual Studio.

To develop Android apps, we need either a Mac or a Windows machine with Xamarin Studio or Visual Studio with the Xamarin.Android plugin.

Xamarin Studio

Xamarin Studio is an IDE from Xamarin. We can download it from `http://xamarin.com/download`.

Xamarin offers different options in its store. To check the version and the plan we need, we can visit `http://store.xamarin.com`.

The editor

The following screenshot shows Xamarin Studio on Mac OS:

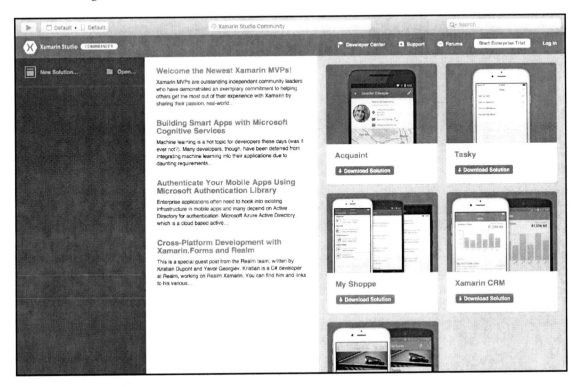

Xamarin Studio could change design in the future, but currently, when we start Xamarin for the first time, we are presented with three areas. Our most recent projects opened are presented on the left. The news from the Xamarin blog is presented in the central area. A list of examples is presented on the right side and we can download, explore, and run them on our devices.

At the top of the left panel are presented the buttons to create a new solution or open an existing one.

A solution is a container for the collection of projects we need to write in order to develop our apps. We will explore in the next chapter all the details of the available project types we can create with Xamarin.

Our focus is now on what Xamarin Studio offers and how we can use this editor in order to work more quickly and more efficiently, taking advantage of all its features.

We can now start developing our first solution:

1. Click on the **File** | **New** | **Solution**.
2. On the left side list, select **Android** | **App**.
3. Click on **Next**.

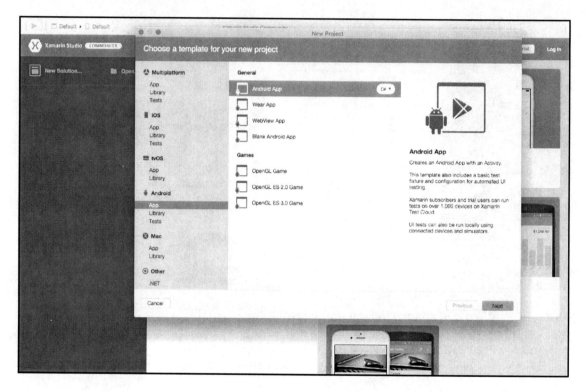

4. Write `XamarinByExample` in the empty field called **App Name**.

5. Click on **Next**:

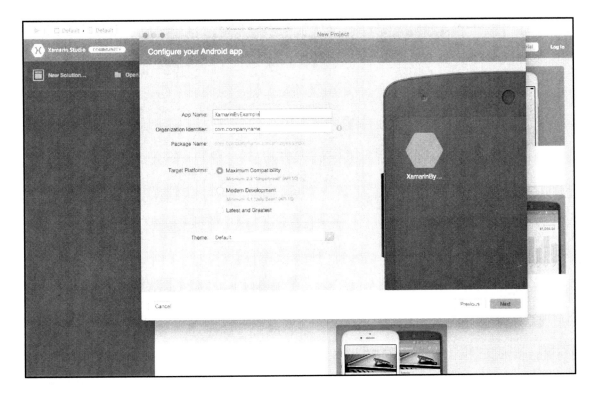

6. Check summary page and click on **Create**:

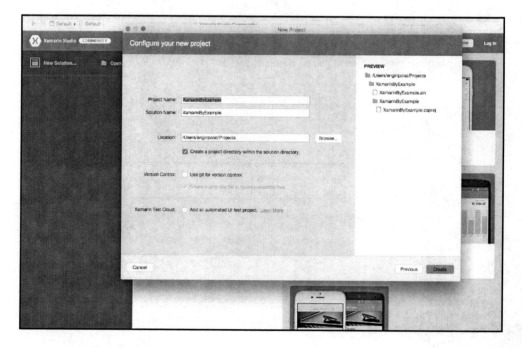

The Xamarin Studio template automatically adds the following to the project:

- References to the libraries `Mono.Android`, `System`, `System.Core`, and `System.Xml`.
- The `Resources` folder with all the base resources the simple app needs
- A file named `MainActivity.cs` that is the main point of access to the app
- The `Assets` folder
- The `Properties` folder

More libraries can be referenced manually by double clicking the References folder on the **Solution** pad.

Adding an iOS project allows us to see one initial difference:

1. Right-click on the **Solution**.
2. Select **Add | New Project**.
3. In the left side list, select **iOS | App**. In the central list, select **Single View App**.
4. Write XamarinByExample.iOS in the empty field called **App Name**.

The Xamarin Studio template creates for us a new iOS project with a simple *Hello world* app.

It automatically adds the following to the project:

- The references to the libraries Xamarin.iOS, System, System.Core, and System.Xml
- The Resources folder
- AppDelegate.cs: The class responsible for launching the UI of application, as well as listening (and optionally responding) to application events from iOS
- Entitlements.plist: The file that configures the permissions on iOS
- Info.plist: The file that configures the entire app
- Main.cs: The entry point of the application
- MainStoryboard.storyboard: The file with the UI storyboard
- XamarinByExample.iOSViewController.cs: This is the ViewController that manages the page designed in the storyboard

Right now we are going to focus on the editor:

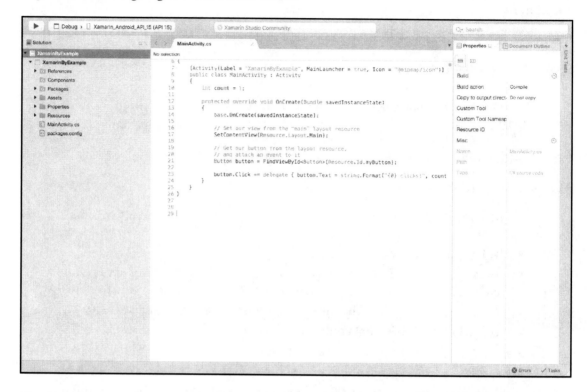

The first button in the top bar is the **Run** button. When we click it, our app runs with the Configuration (Debug, Release) selected in the combo named Configuration selector.

We can select where to run our app using the target selector. The target selector is a combo that contains the list of available devices. They may be either real devices plugged to our machine or virtual devices configured to run in a simulator.

On the top in the center we have the **Notification Area**. Here we can be notified about the numbers of warnings or errors in our app, or the results in a search.

When we click on the **Notification Area**, Xamarin opens up the associated details pad to show us more details of the selected notification.

In the top right section, we find the **Global Search** field.

This is a very useful feature of Xamarin, and we are going to explore it in more detail.

The left-hand section is called the **Solution** pad, and it contains all the files in our solution.

The central section contains the Document. When we open a file from the **Solution** pad, it gets displayed, if possible, in this section.

To zoom in and out the content, use the short keys *Ctrl* + or Ctrl – in Windows and *command* + or *command* – in Mac.

The right-hand section contains the properties and hidden pads that we can customize.

To hide a panel, double-click on its title.

We can customize most of what we've seen so far.

The global search

The global search is one of the most powerful features of the editor.

It allows us to easily jump to the point of the code we need to retrieve.

Go to is the main feature of the global search, and this allows us to find a type, a file, or a declaration.

All we need to write is `type:NameOfTheTypeWeAreLookingFor` and we will be directed to the type.

Using the global search, we can write in the filter just the uppercase letter of the object in camel case we are looking for. So for example, if we are looking for the file `MainActivity.cs`, we can just write `file:MA` and the file will appear on the list eventually with all the others compliant with our filter.

When we are in a file, we can jump to a known line by typing in the global search `:NumberOfLine:NumberOfColumn`.

For example, `:10:10` jumps to the 10th line and 10th column of the document.

The key bindings

The key bindings is a feature that allows us to use short key combinations for actions.

In the following table, we can have a look at some of them:

Short key	Description
⌘ + *D*	This generates the constructor of the class.
cw	`Console.Writeline`.
switch	Template for the `switch` statement.
exception	Template for an entire class exception.
prop	Template for a short property. If we need a private set, we can use `propg`.
try	Template for `try...catch`.

In the menu **Tools** | **Options** (Windows) or **Xamarin Studio** | **Preferences** (Mac), in the section **Environment** | **Key Bindings** we can look at all the default short keys and we can also define ours.

Policies

Xamarin Studio allows us to customize how the code will be automatically formatted.

We will find this feature very useful when we want to be consistent with the coding standard of our company or the coding standards of our customer.

To customize it, we go to **Tools** | **Options** (Windows) or **Xamarin Studio** | **Preferences** (Mac) and select in the left menu **Source Code** | **Code Formatting** | **C#**. A drop-down list appears, where we can select the coding style we prefer, or we can also define our own coding standard by going in to the tab **C# Format**. We will now see an example of code with the current coding standard. Clicking on the **Edit** button, we can choose from different layout options for **Indentation, Braces, Blank Lines, Wrapping, White Spaces,** and **New Lines**.

The **Code Formatting** settings are not saved in the solution but in the local settings of Xamarin Studio. If we share our code with another person with different policies, when they open the solution with their customized Xamarin Studio, they will have the option to apply their own policies for the solution or use the project specific user settings.

We can apply our policies to the document with the short key *Ctrl + I*.

Code template

A code template is a block of reusable code that we can insert where we need it in our code. Code templates can be simple or very complex. For example, blocks such as `try...finally` and `if...else` are commonly used, but we could also use code templates to insert entire classes or methods.

To try one of them, we can go to the `Program.cs`, writing in the global search `file:Program.cs` and pressing *Enter*.

Ctrl + *Shift* + *D* (Windows) or *command* + *shift* + *D* (Mac) automatically writes file: in the global search and moves the focus there.

After the `Console.Writeline("Hello World");` we can write `for` and press double *Tab*.

There the following code would automatically appear:

```
for (int i = 0; i < max; i++)
{

}
```

Using the Tab button, we can navigate between two fields, i and max. We can change them with the values we need. By replacing the field i with myIndex, all the i in the template will be updated with the new value. When we arrive at the last editable value, we can press enter and at this point the template will be transformed in to regular code.

The code templates are written with a simple meta-language.

Here is a small list of the code templates we can find useful:

Keyword	Code template
ctor	It generates the constructor of the class.
cw	`Console.WriteLine.`
switch	Template for the `switch` statement.
exception	Template for an entire class `Exception.`
prop	Template for a short property. If we need a private set we can use `propg.`
try	Template for `try...catch.`

As an exercise, we can try all of them in our code. To use them in our code, we need to write the keyword and press double Tab.

There are about 40 templates currently available for C# in Xamarin.

Going to **Tools** | **Options** (Windows) or **Xamarin Studio** | **Preferences** (Mac), under the **Text Editor** section we can find **Code Templates**, with all of them, and details of how they are implemented.

We can also write our own code template.

If we try to add a property by writing in the code prop + double *Tab*, it generates a short property as follows:

```
public object MyProperty {
        get;
        set;
    }
```

This has object and MyProperty as editable.

The implementation of this template in the meta-language is relatively easy.

```
public $type$ $name$ {
    get;
    set;
}
```

The words between the symbol $ are the ones that are editable. We can put them in the code more than once, and when they have different names they can be navigated with the tab button. When they have the same name, the engine repeats for us, in realtime, what we write in the first field with that name.

It would be great and always useful to have a template that writes an extended property like this:

```
private object _myProperty;
public object MyProperty{
  get
  {
    return _myProperty;
  }
  set
  {
    _myProperty = value;
  }
}
```

Unfortunately, there is not a code template like this. The bright side is that we can create it.

Go to **Tools | Options** (Windows) or **Xamarin Studio | Preferences** (Mac), select **Code Templates** from the **Text Editor** section, and press **Add**.

As a shortcut, we can write propex. We need to select C# from the drop-down list called group and text/x-csharp from the drop-down list called mime. As a description, we can write Template for extended properties.

```
private $type$ $name$;
public $type$ $Name${
    get
    {
        return $name$;
    }
    set
    {
        $name$ = value;
    }
}
```

Now in the drop-down list, on the right, we can select three new fields that are all the fields we inserted between the $ symbols.

We can define the default values for `type`, `name`, and `Name`.

After defining the default values for each field, we just need to press **OK** to save the snippet.

Source analysis

This is a very useful feature of Xamarin, disabled by default. When we enable it we have a powerful tool to raise the level of quality of our code.

The source analysis checks code on the fly and warns of potential errors and style violation, suggesting automatic fixes. To enable it, we need to go to **Tools | Options** (Windows) or **Xamarin Studio | Preferences** (Mac) and turn it on from the **Text Analysis** in the **Text Editor** section.

When enabled, we can see markers in the scroll bar. By moving the mouse over them we can see the problems colored by severity. The scroll bar gives us a high level view of the quality of our code. Some of the suggestions are just recommendations, and this doesn't mean that they have to be addressed.

If we click on the marker and press *Alt + Enter*, a list of suggested actions will be shown and we can decide whether or not to automatically fix the issue with the suggested action.

Regions and comments

Regions let us specify a block of code that we can retrieve in the navigation bar at the top left side of our document. In longer code files, it is convenient to separate the code into regions so that we can focus on the part of the file that we are currently working on. The following example shows how to define a region:

```
#region MyClass definition public class
MyClass
{
 static void Main()
 {
 }
}
#endregion
```

A `#region` block must be terminated with a `#endregion` directive.

 To write a region using code template, we can type `#region` and double tab.

In general, we can comment a line in C# by using `//` before the part to comment or `/*` before the first char to comment and `*/` after the last one. In Xamarin Studio, we can also use a particular comment in our code by using `// TODO: our comment`. This will add the line commented on a task list that we will retrieve any time by clicking on the button **Tasks** positioned at the bottom right of Xamarin Studio.

To comment our classes and fields we use the documentation tags.

The documentation tags are comments in XML that can be useful if we want to automate the technical documentation of our app. The documentation tags are defined using `///` and XML markup.

Xamarin generates the documentation tags for us. The quality of the auto-generated documentation tags is related to the quality of the coding standards we use.

Let's add, for example, a method to `Program.cs` called `TransformTextInLowercase` that transforms a string in its lowercase:

```
string TransformTextInLowercase(string textToTransform)
{
    return textToTransform.ToLower();
}
```

Adding the `///` in the row before the first one and pressing enter allows Xamarin Studio to generate the following comment for us:

```
/// <summary>
/// Transforms the text in lowercase.
/// </summary>
/// <returns>The text in lowercase.</returns>
/// <param name="textToTransform">Text to transform.</param>
string TransformTextInLowercase ( string textToTransform)
{
    return textToTransform.ToLower();
}
```

Xamarin and the Microsoft C# compiler provide us with a way to extract the documentation from the comments.

It looks for XML documentation comments within the source code (comments that start with three slashes, ///), and puts them all into a single XML file.

To auto generate this XML file, we have to:

- Double-click on the name of the project in the solution pad. This opens the properties of the project.
- Click on **Compiler** under the **Build** section on the left side list.
- Flag **Generate xml documentation**.
- Choose a folder and a filename.
- Press the **OK** button.

Next time we compile, a new XML file that contains all the documentation tags will be automatically generated in the deployment folder.

The xml file can be used as the starting point to generate automatic documentation. We can write an xsl to present the data in html, or use tools such as NDoc, Monodoc, or Sandcastle to build a *help* file.

Mobile Development Software Development Lifecycle

A **Mobile Development Software Development Lifecycle** (SDLC) is composed of distinct work phases used to plan, design, build, test, and deliver a mobile app.

An SDLC aims to produce high quality apps that meet or exceed our customer expectations.

We need to base our apps on customer requirements. To do that, it helps to move through clearly defined phases, and prepare scheduled time-frames and accurate cost estimates:

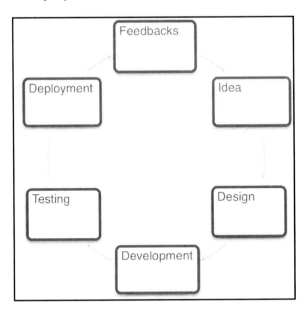

Usually there are six major phases:

- **Idea**: All apps start with an idea. That idea is usually refined throughout the entire SDLC process.
- **Design**: In this phase we define the general layout and how it works. It usually starts by defining the **User Experience (UX)**, converted into a UI design.
- **Development**: This phase is the most intensive for us. In this phase we build the application.
- **Testing**: When the development phase is far enough along, we can release a test application to the QA or test users. This allows us to address possible issues that our app might contain. Testing early is good for our products. Some software development methodologies are driven by testing, or include feature based testing as soon as a feature is available.
- **Deployment**: This releases the app to the stores, or in some of the preview environments available.

- **Feedback**: In this phase, we collect opinions on the app, and based on them, start the process again. This is an important and often under evaluated phase. Listening to our final users is always more important than the technology we use.

These phases often overlap. For example, it is common to start development before the design is finished, or start testing before the development is at a good point but not completed yet.

Idea

Ideas are cheap! Execution is worth millions! Walking on the streets of San Francisco, you will hear that many times. It is actually pretty true. Ideas are cheap.

Potentially everyone has a brilliant idea for the next killer app!

Defining an idea is a key phase in creating a successful app. It is only a small step compared to the execution but it is an important step. Having a clear idea helps us to have clarity from the beginning about what we need to do to transform the idea into reality.

It is all about asking and replying to fundamental questions driven by the market.

To define an idea, we can create our own template in order to have the big picture of the overall app.

In the following table, I am including questions I usually need in order to understand what I am going to develop and why.

We can copy, fill, and pin it in front of us in order to not lose focus during all the phases of the SDLC:

Question	Answer
Are there similar apps? If so, how does the idea of the application differentiate from the others?	
Will the application integrate with or extend the existing infrastructure? If so, what kind of infrastructure needs to be extended or integrated by the app?	
What value does this app bring to users?	
How can I add value using mobile technologies such as location awareness, the camera, and so on?	

This table can obviously grow. The experience will always suggest new questions to us.

An idea sets one or more goals.

When we have the list of goals, we can think about all the steps the user needs to take in order to achieve each one of them. The user is called the *Actor*. Sometime an actor can be another system connected to our app.

The steps the *Actor* needs to take to achieve a goal are called the *usecase.*

Defining *Actors* and usecases tells us what the requirement specifications are.

After that, we can focus on how to design a technical solution that covers the requirement specifications.

Design

When we know what is needed, we can start to think about UX and UI.

User experience design

The UX design is the process of maximizing the usability and the interaction between the user and the application.

This is usually done using mockups and wireframes that may be created even with low tech tools: pencil and paper. But don't worry, that is not the only way! There are tools such as Balsamiq and InVisio that help UX designers to define mockups, providing a first feeling of the app.

This helps to define the interactions and the placeholders before starting the UI design.

User experience is not cross-platform.

When designing the user experience, it is important to consider the interface guidelines for each of the platforms we are designing for.

By following the platform-specific guidelines, we can ensure that our apps are well integrated on the operating system where they are running:

- **Apple**: Human Interface Guidelines – `http://goo.gl/Mi3HPL`
- **Android**: Design Guidelines – `http://goo.gl/LA3fYh`
- **Windows**: Design library for Windows Phone – `http://goo.gl/FQ4IW6`

For example, each platform has its own way to switch between sections, to manage images, and so on. Even the available hardware influences the user expectations for our app. For example, Android devices have a back button, while iOS users expect to have a button in the UI that drives them back to the previous section and the only button is expected to go to the main screen.

User Interface design

UI design transforms the mockups into graphics elements. Spending time on a good UI design is always a good investment. Consider that the most popular apps generally also have great designs and usability.

A well-designed app usually looks different on each platform. As for the UX, it's important to understand that each platform has its own design language.

One example of these differences is the dimension of icons and images that we need in order to see them sharply and crisply on each supported platform.

Development

Development often starts with a proof of concept that validates functionality.

The rest of the book will focus on this phase.

Testing

This is the process of finding and working out the bugs in our app.

Testing generally includes usability and design reviews.

This phase is the overall test of the app, and generally the application follows different stages:

- **Proof of Concept**: Only the core functionality is working and major bugs are present.
- **Alpha**: Core functionality is code-complete and not fully tested. Major bugs are still present and some features may still not be available.

- **Beta**: Most of the functionality is complete. Known issues are present. The app has had some testing and bug fixing.
- **Release candidate**: All functionality is complete and tested. The app is ready to be published.

Xamarin provides a powerful testing framework called Xamarin Test Cloud. This allows us to write automated UI testing.

During development, we can write small tests to check single functionalities (unit testing). We will experience how to develop testing with C# and NUnit later in the book.

In general, the sooner the app is tested, the earlier we can address the issues. For example, if a major issue is found in the proof of concept, the UX of the app can be still modified to address it.

There are different tools to support the distribution in the test phase:

- **TestFairy** (http://testfairy.com/): Supports Android and iOS apps
- **HockeyApp** (http://hockeyapp.net/): Supports Android, iOS, and Windows apps
- **Raygun.IO** (https://raygun.io/): Supports Android, iOS, and Windows apps

Xamarin Insights (https://xamarin.com/insights) is a technology presented in 2014 and designed to bring analytics and crash reporting to our mobile app. It is a real-time monitoring system that enables us to identify, report, and track issues that are impacting users with a simple and effective API.

We will explore the features of Xamarin Insight later in the book.

Deployment

Once our application is stable enough, we can publish it. The deployment is a platform specific step. The distribution options depend on the platform. We will explore an example of deployment in the last chapter of this book. For now, we will have a quick overview of the options.

Distributing through Apple Connect

Apple iOS apps are distributed to the Apple "App Store" via "Apple Connect".

When we submit an App to Apple Connect, we have to wait for a validation. Usually Apple is very strict with the validation process and it can take some weeks.

If our app is not compliant with all the Apple guidelines, it will be rejected with a list of issues to address in order to be compliant.

The Apple Store is the most popular distribution method for iOS applications, and it allows us to market and distribute our apps online with very little effort.

The second type of deployment is the *enterprise deployment*.

This is used for internal distribution of corporate applications that aren't available via the App Store.

A deployment also exists that is intended primarily for development and testing: "ad-hoc deployment".

 When we deploy to a device via Xcode or Xamarin Studio, it is known as ad-hoc deployment.

Distributing through Google Play

The official app store for Android is Google Play, but as we will see, there are a few other different stores that we can consider.

Android is also open to app distribution. Devices are not locked to a single, approved app store.

Anyone is free to create an app store, and most Android phones allow apps to be installed from these third-party stores.

This allows us a potentially larger distribution channel for our applications.

Distributing through Windows Store

Windows Phone applications are distributed to users via the Windows Store.

We need to submit our apps to the Windows Phone Dev Center for approval, after which they appear in the Store. When we submit our apps to the Windows Store, we can also provide an install link to the testers before the app is reviewed and published.

Feedback

During the development cycle we need to collect feedback from the test users.

At this stage we might have usability reviews and functionality reviews.

We will understand our customer better, and what is needed to add value to our app.

Summary

In this chapter, we've started our journey towards learning what mobile cross-platform means, and how to start using Xamarin Studio and its features in order to write our apps with C#.

We prepared all the basics and tools we need to make our first app.

We overviewed the Software Development Lifecycle for mobile applications.

Now we are ready to start developing with Xamarin Studio.

In cross-platform projects, sharing code between projects is important and there are ways to achieve this goal. We'll examine the aspects and methodologies of sharing code by shared projects in next chapter.

Separation between the UI and code behind it is also important. We'll address the MVVM design pattern and learn it by writing an example library.

2
Sharing Code between Platforms

As we mentioned in the previous chapter, in mobile development there are features that we can share between platforms and features that need to be platform specific.

In this chapter we will explore all the ways we have in Xamarin to share code between platforms.

We will understand and develop a cross-platform pattern called **Model-View-View-Model (MVVM)** that helps us to separate the business and presentation logic of our application from its user interface. We will use this paradigm in the rest of the book.

The business logic is the part of a program that determines how data can be displayed, stored, created and changed.

The presentation logic is the part of the program that describes how and when business objects are displayed.

MVVM will help us to make our application easier to test, maintain and evolve. It also improves the amount of code we can share between platforms.

It is important to understand that MVVM and separated logics is not the only way to share the code between different platforms. That's the reason why we are going to have a quick overview of the other possibilities we have.

Shared Project

A Shared Project is a project that contains common code that can be linked to each platform specific library or app. It is compiled as part of the platform specific code.

To develop a nice solution based on a shared project, we need to architect it in order to have the core features in the shared project. We may possibly be using partial classes, abstract classes and interfaces in order to manage the objects that are specific for each platform in the platform specific project.

These kinds of projects are good when we are in a prototype phase, because it is relatively fast to implement a shareable project for the common code and use all the advantages given by the platform specific frameworks.

It's easy to choose a Shared Project approach over PCL when we just develop platform specific applications. A Shared Project allow us to write code to be copied to each project in the solution during compilation. In that way, we can store codes outside the platform specific project and easily translate it when we need to support more platforms. A well-architected shared project will give us more advantages than a platform specific constrained project.

Here is how we create a Shared project:

1. Right-click on the solution and go to **Add** | **New Project**.
2. On the left side, select **Multiplatform** | **Library**.
3. On the right side, select **Shared Project**.
4. Click on **Next**.

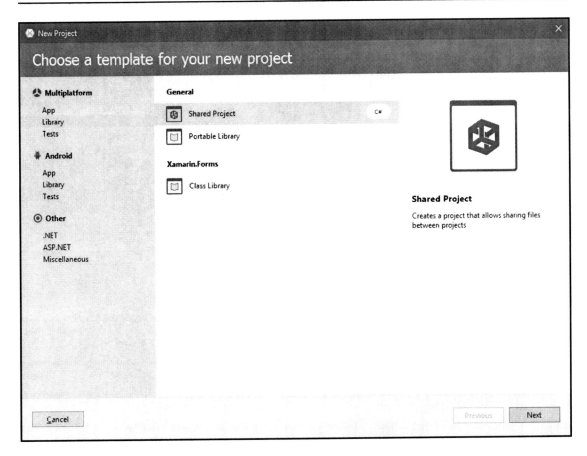

As we can see in the following screenshot, we filled in the **Project Name** box and the **Location** box will have autocompleted:

5. Write `BusinessLayer` in the empty field called **Project Name**.
6. Check summary view of project.

7. Click on **Create**.

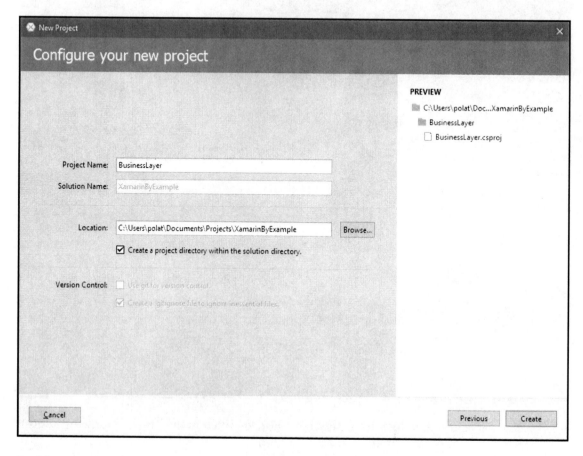

In this way, we can then reference the Shared Project from the platform specific project and all the classes will be available on our platform specific project. The reference to a Shared Project doesn't import a compiled library into our platform specific project. All the files will be compiled in our platform specific project as though they were written there. For this reason, it is important to not write any platform specific code in the Shared Project. Some people do this using the conditional directives `#If PLATFORM` *then*.

To keep the code clean and maintainable, don't do it.

This statement `if` is often avoidable and mostly bad in software development. We usually use the `if` statement when we are too lazy to think and it often creates a lot of damage in our code. `if` can be addictive, so when we start using it we think we cannot get rid of it and we usually tend to abuse the use of statement. A `less-if` code makes our code more readable and maintainable. We can avoid using most of the `if` we write in our code using polymorphism. In this book we will use `if` less, so that we can also learn the concept of `less-if`.

Example an extension method to translate text

As we have seen in the previous chapter, every app should follow a software development life cycle. Every single example we are going to develop in this book starts with an idea and follows at least one fully.

Idea

An extension method of the type string that translates a key into a value loaded from a text file. The text file will be named after a language ISO code (like en-GB). When we ask for a translation of a file that is not available, the default text file will be the source of the translation.

Extension methods enable us to "add" methods to existing types without modifying the original type. We will see in the development of this example how to write an extension method for the type string.

We can now complete our survey in order to understand if we are doing something valuable and how to proceed with the design of it:

Question	Answer
Are there similar apps? If so, how does the idea of the application differentiate from others?	Yes, each platform has its own internationalization paradigms. We want to centralize the translations in one single set of files.
Will the application integrate with or extend existing infrastructure? If so, what kind of infrastructure needs to be extended or integrated by the app?	It will extend each app we are going to develop.
What value does this app bring to users?	Users are developers. It will allow them to have a single translation file consumable by all the platform specific apps.
How can I add value using mobile technologies such as location awareness, the camera, and so on?	We can use the default language of the device in order to select the translation file.

Design

Our users are, in this case, developers. In order to make this component usable we want developers to write as little code as possible to have the maximum value from it.

Another stakeholder of our component would be the person who's going to translate the resources for us. We want them to easily translate the resources and to easily provide us the file we need in the right format.

The content of the file will be a comma separated value file:

```
KEY_OF_VALUE_1,Value 1
KEY_OF_VALUE_2,Value 2
```

The name of the files will be:

```
Default.csv
EN-GB.csv
```

The `csv` format is a standard format that can be edited using the most popular editors of spreadsheets. We use it so the editors can easily read and modify them, providing us with the translations.

From the developers' point of view we want the developers to be able to write something like:

```
string translatedValue = "KEY_OF_VALUE_1".Translate();
```

in order to have the translation of `"KEY_VALUE_1"` in the default language of the phone.

Development

First of all, let's open Xamarin Studio and create a new solution. Select **Multiplatform | Library** on the left side and **Shared Project** on the right side then click **Next**.

For the project name we can assign `XamarinByExample.Chapter2.TranslatorShared`; and for the solution name let's assign `XamarinByExample.Chapter2`; click on **Create**.

Let's delete the class that Xamarin creates for us called `MyClass.cs`. We don't need it. To delete it, right-click on the name in the **Solution** pad and select the **Remove** option. A popup will appear asking us if we want to remove it only from the project or also from the disk. In this case, we want to remove it everywhere so we will select **Delete**.

Now we can right click on the project `XamarinByExample.Chapter2.TranslatorShared` and then **Add | New File**.

In the **Add New File** dialog we can select **General** and the option **Empty class C#**. We will add **Extensions** as the class name and select the **New** button.

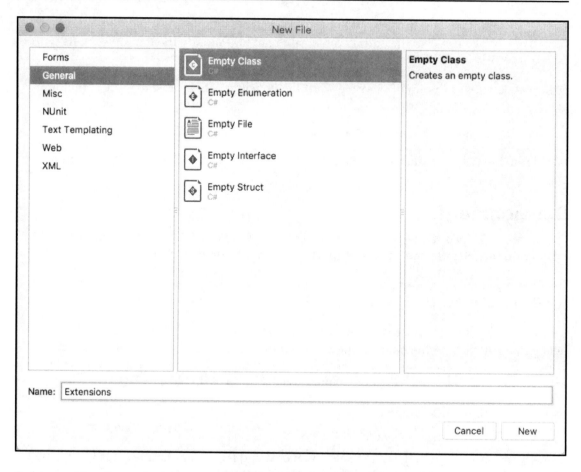

Before writing the code, let's prepare all the files we need. Now we need to have the `default.csv` file to write the default key values we want to use in our apps.

To do that, right-click on the project `XamarinByExample.Chapter2.TranslatorShared` and then **Add | New File**.

In the **Add New File** dialog, select **General** and the option **Empty File**. For the name, we can also include the extension, so let's write `default.csv` in the **Name** field and press **New**.

We can now write in the `default.csv`:

```
HELLO_WORLD,Hello World (Translated from default)
```

Now let's double click on the `Extension.cs` in the **Solution** pad.

As you can see, some C# code has already been written for us by Xamarin when we added the file:

```
using System; namespace XamarinByExample.Chapter2.TranslatorShared
{
    public class Extensions
    {
        public Extensions ()
        {
        }
    }
}
```

We are going to change it.

We need to write an extension method for the type string. Extension methods need to be written in a static class and they need to be static methods. So, the first thing we are going to add is the static statement between `public` and `class`; delete the constructor and to add a static method called `Translate` that returns a string; and, in order to extend the type string, have as arguments of the method a string called `key` with the statement `this` before the declaration of it. Inside the method, we are going to return an empty string for now:

```
public static class Extensions
    {
        /// <summary>
        /// Translate the specified key in the language dependent value.
        /// </summary>
        /// <param name="key">Key to translate.</param>
        public static string Translate(this string key)
        {
            //TODO: implement here the logic to
            the key in the value
            return "";
        }
    }
```

When we put a comment with `TODO`: Xamarin automatically creates a task for us in the Task Manager. We can find these tasks in the **Tasks** pad, which we open from the **Tasks** button at the bottom right of Xamarin Studio.

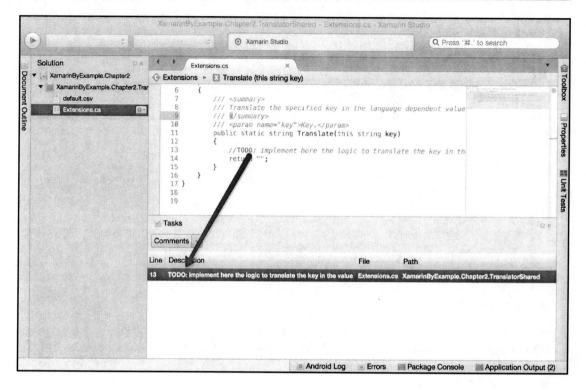

Now let's implement some logic.

First we need to load the resource file from the assembly. Then we need to read the contents of it until we find the correspondent key. When we find it, we will assign the correspondent value to return.

Let's have a look at one possible final implementation of it:

```
/// <summary>
/// Translate the specified key in the language dependent value.
/// </summary>
/// <param name="key">Key to translate</param>
public static string Translate (this string key)
{
        //gets the assembly where this code is compiled
        var assembly = Assembly.GetExecutingAssembly();

      //extracts the namespace of the embedded resource (platform specific)
      var ns = assembly.FullName.Split(new char[]{ ',' }, 2) [0];
      //build the name of the resource using the extracted namespace
      var resourceName = String.Format ("{0}.default.csv", ns) ;
      //define the separator of the csv file
```

```
const char separator = ',';
//assigns the key to the value
var value = key;
// using disposes the objects for us
using (var stream = assembly.GetManifestResourceStream
(resourceName))
using (var reader = new StreamReader (stream)) {
   //read the file till the end and save it in a variable called
result
   var result = reader.ReadToEnd ();
   //build an array where each element is a row of the file
   var lines = result.Split ('\n');
   //iterate until the value has not been replaced
   //or the file has been read till the end.
   //To put the condition inside the statement of the cycle
   //allows us to avoid writing a redundant "if" statements
   inside the cycle
   for (var i = 0; i < lines.Length && value == key; i++) {
      //separate the key from the values using the separator.
      var keyValues = result.Split (new char[]{ separator }, 2);

      // this is a ternary operator (info box)
      value = (keyValues [0] == key) ? keyValues [1] : key;
   }
}
//returns the value that is the same as the key
if nothing has been found
return value;
}
```

A ternary operator is a possible syntax of a conditional expression where:
```
If (a == b) { c } else { d }
```
Is written as:
```
( a == b ) ? c : d
```

We can now add a new iOS and a new Android project and reference the Shared Project in both of them to test this feature.

The only thing to remember is that to reference a Shared Project is like copying the code inside our project. It will be compiled inside the project, and not in the apparent library of the Shared Project. In fact, the Shared Project is not a library at all. It is just a container of code common to different platforms.

To test our project with the apps, we have to add the namespace where the extension method is, and then we can call everywhere we have a type string the `Translate` method and it will use the embedded file to find the correspondent value:

```
"HELLO_WORLD".Translate()
```

In the original idea there was a final requirement "translate into the default language of the phone". Unfortunately, each platform has its own way to save and retrieve the default language of the phone.

We need to find a way to tell the language to the extension method from the platform specific project. The only way that the extension method has to generalize it by itself seems to be the conditional compilation statement `#If PLATFORM`. We do not want to do that, do we?

 To see one possible complete solution to this example, download it at `http://www.enginpolat.com/books/xbe/XamarinByExample.Chapter2-.zip`

Portable Class Library

Portable Class Library (PCL) is a set of platform independent APIs that can be referenced in more than one platform. They are a subset of the .NET **Base Class Library** (BCL).

 .NET BCL is a library that contains the standards of the C# language. It provides types to represent the data types of the Common Language Interface, file access, custom attributes, security attributes, string manipulation, formatting, streams, and collections. It defines types in namespaces we might be familiar with (`System`, `System.Collections`, `System.Collections.Generics`, `System.Diagnostics`, `System.Globalization`, `System.IO`, `System.Security`, `System.Security.Permissions`, `System.Text`, and `System.Threading`)

In a PCL, we need to select a profile that includes a list of targeted platforms. Actually the more platforms we need to support, the smaller is the subset of BCL we can use.

Unlike a Shared project, a PCL generates a compiled library that can be referenced by projects included in the targeted frameworks.

To create a PCL, we can right click on the solution and go to **Add | New Project**.

In the **New Project** dialog, we need to select C# in the left side list and **Portable Library** in the central list.

When a PCL is created in Xamarin Studio it is automatically configured with a profile that works for Xamarin.iOS and Xamarin.Android. We can check the `References` folder in order to see the subset of .NET portable library that we can use in our project.

In the PCL Settings we can define the profile. Double-click the project, and the **Project Options** dialog will appear. In this dialog we can go to **Build | General** and check or change the current profile. Changing any of the **Target Framework** options automatically updates the **Current Profile**.

Once a PCL has been created, we can reference it from any compatible application or library by double clicking on **References** under the tab **Projects**.

This means that we can create our very own PCL plugin. These PCL plugins will allow us to add rich cross platform functionality to Xamarin, Xamarin.Forms and Windows Projects that use a PCL or Shared Project.

A multiplatform PCL connectivity plugin

We are now going to explore the code of a simple cross-platform plugin to check the connection status of a mobile device acquiring additional information such as connection type and bandwidth.

We will develop our own shortly but for now it's worth taking a look and fully understanding something that has been done by the team behind Xamarin. The plugin has been written by James Montemagno. It is available on NuGet and the code has been published at `https://github.com/jamesmontemagno/Xamarin.Plugins`.

NuGet is an open source package manager for the Microsoft development platform. It is fully supported by Xamarin Studio. We'll find several plugins usable from our apps here. To explore them right-click on the name of the project on the **Solution** pad and then **Add | Add Nuget packages…**

Also, Xamarin has its own package repository called **Xamarin Component Library**. We can easily access the Xamarin Component Library from `https://components.xamarin.com/`. There are tons of components and most of them are platform independent. We can find, download, and use them in our projects to add functionality to our projects in minutes. Examples include cloud integration, barcode scanning, charting, themes, and so on.

Idea

The idea is to be able to understand the structure and architecture of an existing plugin in order to invent our own plugin.

The plugin we are going to analyze has been written in order to have a simple interface that works cross platform and allows us to check the connectivity. This feature is going to be really useful in our projects and we will use it later in the book.

Development

We are now starting to explore the development of this plugin. The mentioned link (`https://github.com/jamesmontemagno/Xamarin.Plugins`) contains different plugins but we are going to focus on the project called `Connectivity`.

After downloading them, we can open the file `Connectivity.sln` from the `Connectivity` folder.

As we can see, it is composed of 11 projects:

- `Connectivity.Plugin`
- `Connectivity.Plugin.Abstractions`
- `Connectivity.Plugin.Android`
- `Connectivity.Plugin.iOS`
- `Connectivity.Plugin.iOSUnified`
- `Connectivity.Plugin.Net45`
- `Connectivity.Plugin.UWP`
- `Connectivity.Plugin.WindowsPhone8`
- `Connectivity.Plugin.WindowsPhone81`
- `Connectivity.Plugin.WindowsPhone81SL`
- `Connectivity.Plugin.WindowsStore`

The core project is generally the first one to develop.

In this case, the core project is `Connectivity.Plugin.Abstractions`. We can see it has included a `References` folder in each project. Each project depends on `Connectivity.Plugin.Abstractions` while it has only one dependency to ".NET Portable Subset", which confirms to us that is a PCL project.

Expanding the `Connectivity.Plugin.Abstractions` on the **Solution** pad, we can see the core of the shareable classes. There are three files:

- `IConnectivity.cs`: This is the interface that defines methods, properties and events of the feature that is implemented in the plugin.
- `BaseConnectivity.cs`: This is the abstract class that does some common work, like throwing events or disposing the objects. This class can be inherited from an implementation class on the platform specific project. When a class inherits from an abstract class, we need to implement all the methods and properties defined as virtual on the base class and we have the option to override the methods marked as virtual.
- `ConnectionType.cs`: This is the enumerator that defines a set of items to describe the type of the connection.

The `Connectivity.Plugin` project defines a `CrossConnectivity` class that uses the `Connectivity.Plugin.Abstractions` library and contains the main point of access to the APIs defined there. It is also a PCL library but the file `CrossConnectivity.cs` will be linked to the platform specific projects and this means that this class is going to be compiled directly in the platform specific libraries.

We can now explore the platform specific projects. They all reference the `Connectivity.Plugin.Abstractions` but note that they are not PCL projects any more. They are now using the platform specific core libraries. They all have a customized implementation of the `BaseConnectivity` class that is called with the same name `ConnectivityImplementation` in all of them. This is not mandatory but is a reasonable choice that allows us to have the same semantic structure.

Each `ConnectivityImplementation` class has its own implementation because the ways to check the connectivity differ between Windows, iOS, and Android, but we want to provide a common way to call it from the multiplatform application we want to develop.

Note also how sometimes the implementation of the `BaseConnectivity` is shared. We can look, for example, at `Connectivity.Plugin.iOS` and `Connectivity.Plugin.iOSUnified`. The class `ConnectivityImplementation` that has been written in the `Connectivity.Plugin.iOS` project has been linked to the `Connectivity.Plugin.iOSUnified` project. The difference between `Connectivity.Plugin.iOS` and `Connectivity.Plugin.iOSUnified` is in the referenced classes. `Connectivity.Plugin.iOS` depends on the monotouch core library, which doesn't support 64 bit like the `iOSUnified` that depends on the `Xamarin.iOS` core library. In this case, it is not going to make any difference to the code written for the specific platform, so `Connectivity.Plugin.iOSUnified` contains only classes linked from the `Connectivity.Plugin.iOS` project.

MVVM pattern a quick overview of theory

This book is not about theories. We will explore the world of multiplatform development by examples, making our ideas reality and learning "how to" on the go. The rest of the book will focus on this, but it worth spending a moment to consider the main ideas behind the MVVM pattern and its structure.

The idea behind the MVVM pattern is to separate the data and its logic from the user interface. To do that, we will group the definitions of the entities and the logic to store them in a library we called Model and all the UI related features in another library called **View**. To manage the communication between those two groups, called application layers, we will develop a third library called **ViewModel**:

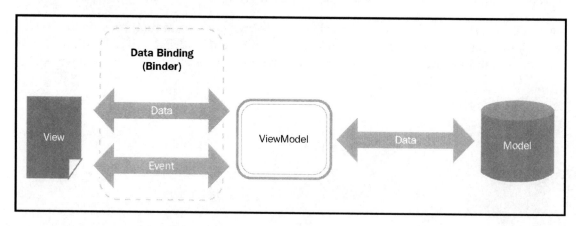

Our components will work together like three teams of people, where the Model groups will have the skills of "what", the ViewModel groups the skills of "when" and the View groups the skills of "how" to present a result to the final user.

Every time we find it difficult to understand which part of the MVVM pattern to put our code in, we will ask ourselves whether the code we are writing is replying to the question "what" (Model), "when" (ViewModel), or "how" (View) to present as a result to the final user.

The communication channels between those three parts are called **Data Binding** and **Commands**.

The power given by this pattern allows us to write the Model and the ViewModel as one single multiplatform library written with shared code or PCL; and to limit to a very small percentage the platform specific code written to support platform specific behaviors related to the UI or the sensors.

In the next chapter, we will explore Xamarin.Forms. Xamarin.Forms is a cross-platform UI toolkit abstraction that allows us to create user interfaces that can be shared across Android, iOS, and Windows Phone. Xamarin.Forms has been written using the MVVM architecture.

MVVM pattern example – split the bill

It's now time to develop our very first cross-platform library.

Idea

The idea is to make a library that allows us to write the total of the bill, the percentage of the total tip and the number of people, giving us the total per person.

Design

At a sketch level, we want a user interface that calculates the bill for each person, having as inputs the current bill, the percentage of tip and the number of people.

Development

Projects with MVVM in mind are normally structured with:

- One shared "core" PCL project containing as much code as possible: models, view models, services, converters, and so on
- One UI project per platform, each containing the bootstrap and view-specific code for that platform

We will start to develop this from the core project, which will contain our Model and ViewModel. We will start the next chapter by analyzing how to use the core library in the platform specific UI.

To create the core, we can use the Xamarin Studio project template **PCL Project**.

The core portable application

First of all, we need to create the core PCL:

1. Click on **New Solution…**.
2. Select **Multiplatform | Library** from the list on the left-hand side.
3. Select **Portable Library** from the central list.
4. Click on **Next**.
5. Write XBE.SplitTheBill.Core in the empty field called **Project Name**.
6. The field **Solution name** contains now the same text we wrote. Let's just replace it with XBE.SplitTheBill.
7. Click on **Create**.

If we now go to check the references using the **Solution** pad, we can apparently see a unique reference called **.NET Portable Subset**. By expanding it we will discover all the referenced libraries supported by the custom profile PCL 4.5 that supports Windows 8, Windows Phone Silverlight 8, Windows Store apps (Windows 8), Xamarin.Android, Xamarin.iOS Classic (deprecated), Xamarin.iOS Unified, and Xamarin.Mac Unified.

The list of libraries under the reference ".NET Portable Subset" are all we can use and share between all the platforms listed by the chosen profile.

> To see, and eventually to change, the current profile, double-click on the name of the project XBE.SplitTheBill.Core from the solution pad and select **Build | General** from the left-hand side list of the **Project Option** dialog.

Now it's time to delete the file MyClass.cs, which was created automatically from Xamarin Studio (we don't need this, do we?).

We will now start to give an architectural shape to our project, adding a folder called Services that will contain our BillCalculatorService:

1. Right-click on the project XBE.SplitTheBill.Core then **Add | New Folder** and rename the folder as Services.
2. Right-click on the folder Services then **Add | New File**.
3. On the **New File** dialog, click on **General** on the left side, select **Empty Interface** from the central list, and write in the **Name** field, the name ISplitBillCalculation.

The interface will define a method called AmountPerPerson that takes as input the total bill, the number of people, and the tip percentage:

```
public interface ISplitBillCalculation {    double AmountPerPerson (double
totalBill, int numberOfPeople, int percentageOfTip); }
```

Now we can implement this interface, creating a class called BillCalculation:

1. Right-click on the folder **Services** then **Add | New File**.
2. On the **New File** dialog, click on **General** on the left side, select **Empty Class** from the central list and write in the **Name** field, the name SplitBillCalculation.

Here, we can implement the interface `ISplitBillCalculation` writing after the definition of the class, the statement : `ISplitBillCalculation`, which in this case is read as `implements ISplitBillCalculation`:

```
public class SplitBillCalculation : ISplitBillCalculation
{
        #region ISplitBillCalculation implementation
        public double AmountPerPerson (double totalBill, int
numberOfPeople,
        int percentageOfTip)
        {
            return ( (totalBill) * ( (double) percentageOfTip / 100 )
            / numberOfPeople );
        }
        #endregion
}
```

Xamarin Studio helps to implement interfaces. As soon as we write the statement `ISplitBillCalculator`, we can go over it with the mouse and a little yellow square will appear under the I. If we click it, we can select the option to prepare the implementation of all the required interfaces for us.

This gives us the business logic for our App. It tells us "what" we need to provide to the final user, so it is part of the Model in the MVVM pattern.

As we've seen, the second part of the Core library should be the ViewModel that tells us "When" to present the data to the final user.

The ViewModel uses the Model to receive and transmit data to the View. In our project the SplitBillViewModel will have as input from the View the total of the bill, the number of people and the tip percentage. It will offer as output to the View the split bill calculated by the SplitBillCalculation service we've developed as a model.

Before coding, we can import now the MVVM Cross Library from NuGet:

1. Right-click on the project title and select **Add** | **Add NuGet Packages...**.
2. On the **NuGet package** dialog write **MvvmCross** in the search field, flag on the **MvvmCross** and click on **Add Packages**.

The MvvmCross library is an open source library that provides us with a framework that implements the MVVM pattern:

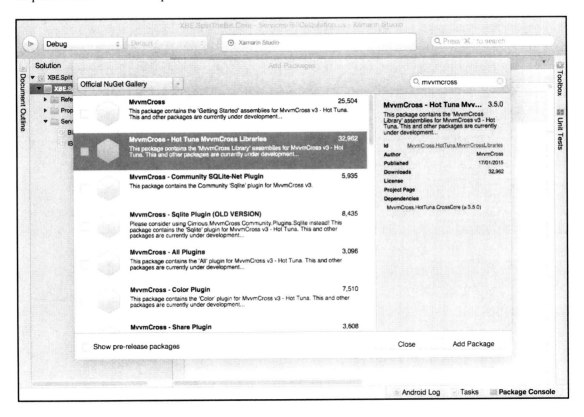

Xamarin Studio adds a new folder called Packages and new references to the References folder, grouped under the name of **From Packages**. We can now create a folder called ViewModels and then the class SplitBillViewModel.

Xamarin Studio creates the class template, which will appear like this:

```
using System; namespace XBE.SplitTheBill.Core {
    public class SplitBillViewModel
    {
        public SplitBillViewModel ()
        {
        }
    }
}
```

To use the MvvmCross Framework we can now add the following using statement to import the namespace we need in order to use the ViewModels APIs:

```
using  MvvmCross.Core.ViewModels;
```

Now we need to inherit, from MvxViewModel, a base abstract class of the MvvmCross framework.

We will also modify the constructor by adding the input parameter, the interface to the IBillCalculation service, and adding a private field to save the value that we will receive as input. Our class now appears like this:

```
using System; using  MvvmCross.Core.ViewModels;
namespace XBE.SplitTheBill.Core {
    public class SplitBillViewModel : MvxViewModel
    {
        readonly ISplitBillCalculation _billCalculation;
        public SplitBillViewModel (ISplitBillCalculation billCalculation)
        {
            _billCalculation = billCalculation;
        }
    }
}
```

ViewModel instances using a 4-step process:

Construction: Using **Inversion of Control (IoC)** for Dependency Injection. The IoC is the process used by a part of the Mvvm framework called ViewLocator that, when the app runs, it finds and creates all the ViewModels resolving the input parameter through the model interfaces in the constructor (our IBillCalculation).

Init(): Initialization of navigation parameters.

ReloadState(): Rehydration after tombstoning .

Start(): Called when initialization and rehydration are complete. We can write class the override of this method in our class in order to initialize our parameters.

In a Calculate method , we'll insert the call to the service we wrote in the Model:

```
void Calculate ()
{
    AmountPerPerson = _billCalculation.AmountPerPerson (TotalBill,
    NumberOfPeople, PercentageOfTip);
}
```

Now we need to define the properties we need and we will call RaisePropertyChanged when a property is set in order to notify the ViewModel that data has changed.

When one of the properties is used to calculate, the result is set, we will also call our Calculate method to refresh the result:

```
double _totalBill;
public double TotalBill {
        get { return _totalBill; }
        set {
            _totalBill = value;
             RaisePropertyChanged (() => TotalBill);
            Calculate ();
        }
    }
    int _numberOfPeople;
    public int NumberOfPeople {
        get { return _numberOfPeople; }
        set {
            _numberOfPeople = value;
             RaisePropertyChanged (() => NumberOfPeople);
            Calculate ();
```

```
        }
    }
    int _percentageOfTip;
    public int PercentageOfTip {
        get { return _percentageOfTip; }
        set {
            _percentageOfTip = value;
            RaisePropertyChanged (() => PercentageOfTip);
            Calculate ();
        }
    }
    double _amountPerPerson;
    public double AmountPerPerson {
        get { return _amountPerPerson; }
        private set {
            _amountPerPerson = value;
            RaisePropertyChanged (() => AmountPerPerson);
        }
    }
}
```

 You can download the complete solution of this example at `http://www.e nginpolat.com/books/xbe/XamarinByExample.Chapter2-1.zip`.

Summary

We have explored the different options we have to create cross-platform libraries using Xamarin.

We've learned how to develop a cross-platform extension method and how to read the code written by others, exploring some of the best practices for developing mobile applications.

We've overviewed Shared Projects, and Portable Class Libraries, and we've overviewed the Model-View-ViewModel Architectural Pattern, and started developing it from the Core library.

Are we ready to explore all of the capabilities that Xamarin.Forms offers us?

In the next chapter, we'll cover all the UI controls, Page types, and Layout types that come with Xamarin.Forms.

Also we'll discover rendering mechanics and the application class in Xamarin.Forms.

3
Exploring the UI Controls

Generally, we need to develop apps for multiple platforms, and often, a mobile project starts with the assumption that an app needs to look the same on each platform.

What is wrong with this approach?

We will discover this later in the chapter as we learn how to use shared code in order to suit platform-specific behaviors.DatePicker is an element that allows the user to input a date with

In `Xamarin.Forms`, UI controls are known as Views. We'll explore Views later in this chapter, starting with Pages and Layouts.

The user's point of view

If we think that a mobile app has to follow the same flow and has to have the same UI on all the available platforms, we are clearly forgetting one of the most important parts of our app: the end users.

We should consider end users as platform-specific entities of our project.

Often, end user is used to a specific operating system and expects to interact with the app in a way that is as close as possible to the most common features that are embedded in the native operating system.

When we explore some of the common embedded apps on each platform, we will see key differences in usability: for instance, in the e-mail app, or in the music app, we might have the same content on iOS, Android, and Windows Phone, but with a different navigation flow and different gestures required to interact with content.

The user's point of view is a platform-specific part of the pattern that is often forgotten. The communication channel between the end user and the app is the **user interface (UI),** and this fact tells us that the UI should be platform-specific since, in general, each user expects to interact with it in a different way.

Xamarin.Forms

Xamarin.Forms is a cross-platform component that allows us to generalize our user interface with C# classes, which are rendered with controls, optimized, and customized on iOS, Android, and Windows Phone.

It provides us a way to write a fully native application that looks and behaves naturally on each of our supported platforms and have a common core code that, in general, allows us to write less platform-specific code.

`Xamarin.Forms` transforms the common code to platform-specific features using the Rendering Model.

Rendering Model

`Xamarin.Forms` has common APIs to describe cross-platform mobile user interfaces.

The description of the UI is categorized by pages, layouts, and controls. We will explore each one of them in this chapter.

Each page, layout, and control is rendered differently on each platform using a Renderer class.

A renderer creates a native control corresponding to the `Xamarin.Forms` representation, arranges it on the screen, and adds the behavior specified in the shared code.

In this chapter, we will implement our own custom Renderer class to customize the appearance and behavior of a control.

Custom renderers for a given type can be added to one application project to customize the control in one platform while allowing the default behavior on other platforms.

Custom renderers can be added to each application project to create a different look and feel on iOS, Android, and Windows Phone.

The Application class

Xamarin.Forms introduces a base Application class.

The Application class contains three virtual methods that can be overridden to handle lifecycle methods:

- OnStart: This method is called when the application starts.
- OnSleep: This method is called each time the application goes to the background. When the application naturally terminates, this is the last notification we will receive.
- OnResume: This method is called when the application is resumed, after being retrieved from the background to foreground.

The Application class contains a property called Properties that is a dictionary, which stores simple values across the app. This dictionary is also persisted in the memory so it will be available even after we restart the app.

The Application class will be created automatically when we create a new Xamarin.Forms project.

To check the order of the calls we can put a Debug.WriteLine call in each one of the lifecycle methods:

```
protected override void OnStart ()
{
        Debug.WriteLine ("OnStart");
}

protected override void OnSleep ()
{
        Debug.WriteLine ("OnSleep");
}

protected override void OnResume ()
{
        Debug.WriteLine ("OnResume");
}
```

The Properties dictionary

We can use the `Properties` dictionary to store or read data in the `OnStart`, `OnSleep`, and `OnResume` methods and from anywhere in our `Xamarin.Forms` code.

The `Properties` dictionary uses a string key and stores an object value.

For example, we could set an `ID` property anywhere in our code, like this:

```
Application.Current.Properties["id"] = someClass.ID;
```

The `Properties` dictionary stores objects so we need to cast its value before using it:

```
if ( Application.Current.Properties.ContainsKey("id") )
{
  int id = (int)Application.Current.Properties["id"];
}
```

We always need to check for the presence of the key before accessing it to prevent unexpected errors.

The `Properties` dictionary is saved to the device.

Data added to the dictionary will be available when the application returns from the background or even after it is restarted.

`Xamarin.Forms` provides the `Application.Current.Properties` dictionary to store persisted data across reruns of the application. It saves all contained data during the `OnSleep` event. If our application doesn't hit the `OnSleep` event (if it crashes, and so on), data won't save, so we should call the `Application.Current.SavePropertiesAsync();` method to force save.

On the other hand, the `FileSystem.Current.LocalStorage` property returns an `IFolder` object to access files and folders that can only be accessed by our application. We can serialize or deserialize any variable inside of a file and write it to the `LocalStorage` folder.

The third option when persisting data between application reruns is the SQLite database. Xamarin has an SQLite.Net Nuget package to access, read, insert, update, and delete any data inside of an Sqlite database. We just have to create the database file and the tables inside of it and store or query data.

The MainPage property

The MainPage property on the Application class sets the root page of the application.

For example, we can create logic in our Application class to display a different page depending on whether the user is logged in or not.

The MainPage property should be set in the App constructor:

```
public class App : Xamarin.Forms.Application
{
    public App ()
    {
        MainPage = new ContentPage {
          Title = "Sample"
        };
    }
}
```

This class is then instantiated in each platform-specific project and passed to a LoadApplication method, which is where the MainPage is loaded and displayed to the user.

The C# inherits from the FormsApplicationPage class and calls LoadApplication to create an instance of our Xamarin.Forms app.

 It is good practice to explicitly use the application namespace to qualify the app because Windows Phone applications also have their own Application class, which is unrelated to Xamarin.Forms

Pages

The Page class is a visual element that occupies part or all of a screen and contains a single child. A Xamarin.Forms.Page represents an Activity in Android, a View Controller in iOS, or a Page in Windows Phone.

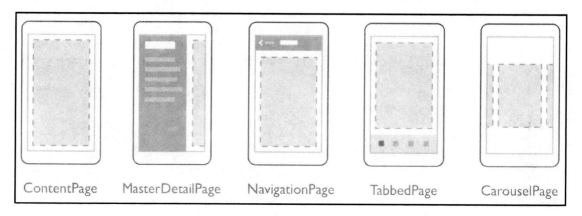

ContentPage   MasterDetailPage   NavigationPage   TabbedPage   CarouselPage

ContentPage

These page are created when a user clicks on our menu items.

They display a single view that often contains a StackLayout or ScrollView, which we will analyze shortly.

To define a content page, we need to use the following line of code:

```
using Xamarin.Forms;
```

Then inherit from ContentPage:

```
public class MonkeyContractsPage : ContentPage
{
  public MonkeyContractsPage (){}
}
public class MonkeyLeadsPage : ContentPage
{
  public MonkeyLeadsPage (){}
}
public class MonkeyAccountsPage : ContentPage
{
  public MonkeyAccountsPage (){}
```

```
}
public class MonkeyOpportunitiesPage : ContentPage
{
   public MonkeyOpportunitiesPage (){}
}
```

The appearances on the three platforms are basically the same since this is a simple page with content.

MasterDetailPage

MasterDetailPage manages two panes of information:

- A master page that presents data at a high level
- A detail page that displays low-level details about information in the master

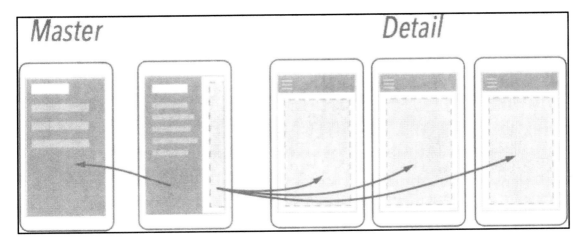

Think of MasterDetailPage as the remote controller of our application navigation. When a user clicks on the menu icon, MasterDetail pushes the menu onto the screen. Then, when the user taps on a menu item, MasterDetail creates the target page and pushes it onto the stack.

To create it, we need to define the following:

- Menu page
- Menu items
- Content pages
- Menu list data
- Menu list view
- Root page

Menu page

The menu page is a `Xamarin.Forms` page that will be shown when the user clicks the menu button.

In this example, our `MenuPage` is a simple content page with a `StackLayout` containing a label and a `ListView` of our menu items:

```
public class MonkeyMenuPage : ContentPage
{
  public ListView MonkeyMenu { get; set; }
  public MonkeyMenuPage ()
  {
    Icon = "ourMenuButton.png";
    Title = "menu"; // The Title property must be set. If we don't the
    application will throw an error

    MonkeyMenu = new MenuListView ();
    var menuLabel = new ContentView {
      Content = new Label {
        Text = "MENU"
      }
    };
    var layout = new StackLayout {
      Spacing = 0,
      VerticalOptions = LayoutOptions.FillAndExpand
    };

    layout.Children.Add (menuLabel);
    layout.Children.Add (MonkeyMenu);
    Content = layout;
  }
}
```

The public property `MonkeyMenu` is a ListView that allows our `MasterDetail` page access to the `ItemSelected` event. When the event is fired, the item selected will be sent to the `NavigateTo` method on the master detail object.

Menu item

Menu items will contain our menu data. The most important data type is Target.

When a user clicks on a menu item, the `NavigateTo` method will create a new page from `TargetType` and push that page onto the stack:

```
public class MonkeyMenuItem
{
    public string Title { get; set; }

    public string IconSource { get; set; }

    public Type TargetType { get; set; }
}
```

Content pages

We can create three pages, which we will call Species, History, and Settings, where we can put the content we want to see in the detail page.

If we right-click on the project and click on the **New File** menu item, the **New File** dialog will open. We can select **Cross-Platform** on the left-hand list and select **Forms ContentPage** on the right-hand list and name it as **SpeciesPage**, shown as follows:

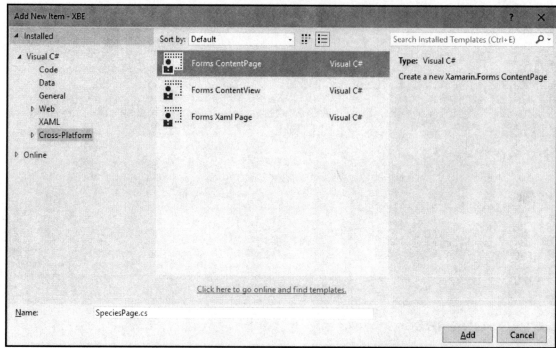

This will create a `hello world` page for us to show a simple message on screen.

The `SpeciesPage` will appear like this:

```
using Xamarin.Forms;

namespace XBE
{
    public class SpeciesPage : ContentPage
    {
        public SpeciesPage  ()
        {
            Content = new StackLayout {
                Children = {
                    new Label { Text = "Hello ContentPage" }
                }
            };
        }
    }
}
```

You may also add `HistoryPage` and `SettingsPage` and continue to the next step.

MenuListData

The `MenuListData` class is the data structure that contains our application's navigation.

We can get this data from the database or configuration file.

The menu structure of this example is done by adding the code below to the list of pages we want to show:

```
public class MonkeyMenuListData : List<MonkeyMenuItem>
    {
        public MonkeyMenuListData ()
        {
            this.Add (new MonkeyMenuItem () {
                Title = "Species",
                IconSource = "species.png",
                TargetType = typeof(SpeciesPage)
            });

            this.Add (new MenuItem () {
                Title = "History",
                IconSource = "history.png",
                TargetType = typeof(HistoryPage)
            });

            this.Add (new MenuItem () {
                Title = "Settings",
                IconSource = "settings.png",
                TargetType = typeof(SettingsPage)
            });
        }
    }
```

Menu List View

The menu list models the ListView defining the appearance of the cells:

```
public class DrawerMenuListView : ListView
{
  public MonkeyMenuListView ()
        {
              List<MonkeyMenuItem> data = new MonkeyMenuListData ();

              ItemsSource = data;
              VerticalOptions = LayoutOptions.FillAndExpand;
              BackgroundColor = Color.Transparent;

              var cell = new DataTemplate (typeof(ImageCell));
              cell.SetBinding (TextCell.TextProperty, "Title");
        }
}
```

Root page

The root page needs to inherit from MasterDetailPage and set in the constructor the initialization of the view. We can set the instance of MonkeyMenu as Master and the first page we want to show (SpeciesPage) as Detail:

```
using Xamarin.Forms;

namespace XBE
{
    public class RootPage : MasterDetailPage
    {
        public RootPage ()
        {
            var menuPage = new MonkeyMenu ();

            menuPage.Menu.ItemSelected += (sender, e) =>
            NavigateTo (e.SelectedItem as MonkeyMenuItem);

            Master = menuPage;
            Detail = new NavigationPage (new SpeciesPage ());
        }

        void NavigateTo (MonkeyMenuItem menu)
        {
            Page displayPage = (Page)Activator.CreateInstance
            (menu.TargetType);
```

```
        Detail = new NavigationPage (displayPage);

        IsPresented = false;
    }
  }
}
```

If we set the root page as the main page in the application file, we can already deploy it on our cross platform devices.

The constructor of our app should now appear like this:

```
public App ()
{
    // The root page of your application
    MainPage = new RootPage ();
}
```

NavigationPage

`NavigationPage` is a page that manages users' navigation in a stack. A navigation page implements the interface INavigation.

With access to the INavigation interface, our page can do things like push and pop new pages on the stack, push and pop modal pages, reshuffle the stack of pages, or remove everything from the stack except the root page:

```
public interface INavigation
{
Task PushAsync(Page page);
Task<Page> PopAsync();
Task PopToRootAsync();
Task PushModalAsync(Page page);
Task<Page> PopModalAsync();
}
```

To start the navigation stack, we have to pass a `ContentPage` into the `NavigationPage` constructor.

The first page added to `NavigationPage` is called the `rootPage` of the navigation stack:

```
ContentPage rootPage = new ContentPage();
var myNavigationPage = new NavigationPage( rootPage );
```

It is very important to construct the `NavigationPage` with the root page, and we cannot forget this step otherwise the app will crash as soon as the `NavigationPage` is called.

Push and Pop

We can use the push and pop methods of the INavigation interface to navigate between different pages. Calling those methods creates a stack of pages. When we call the push methods, a page will be added on top of this stack making the stack bigger. It's very important to pop in order to remove the page from the stack when we want to go back to other pages. On the navigation pages, the back button will pop the current page from the stack revealing the page beneath it.

When we pop all the pages and we arrive in the root page, the back button will not be available and the pop methods cannot be used. In the INavigation interface, there is also a pop to root method that will remove all the pages of the stack except the root page.

 Both pop and push methods to the navigation stack is made asynchronously. Asynchronous calls (such as `PushAsync`, `PopAsync`, and so on) run without blocking the CPU until they finish. This makes application runs fluent, even if the job takes a long time to complete. The CPU may continue to execute other tasks while asynchronous tasks are running. Typically, the CPU continuously executes tasks, but some tasks takes longer to finish and the CPU starts to wait for them. In this situation, the CPU does nothing and the device spends precious CPU cycles for nothing. With the asynchronous approach, the CPU has to wait for a task's finish signal before it starts to execute other tasks.

TabbedPage

`TabbedPage` displays an array of tabs, each of which loads content onto the screen.

The default appearance of the tab is platform-specific. If we want to customize them, we need to write our own custom renderer. We will see how to customize the controls using custom renderers in `Chapter 6`, *Custom Renderers*.

To create `TabbedPage`, we need to prepare the content pages to add to it.

When we have them, we can add a new C# file called, for example, `TabbedRootPage`, and inherit from `TabbedPage`. On the constructor we can now add to the `Children` property the pages we want, and they will be reachable by the user by just touching the title of the page in the `TabBar` on the screen:

```
public class TabbedRootPage : TabbedPage
{
    public TabbedRootPage ()
    {
        SendPageMenu sendPage = new SendPageMenu();
        LivePageMenu livePage = new LivePageMenu ();
        InboxPageMenu inboxPage = new InboxPageMenu ();
        InvitePageMenu invitePage = new InvitePageMenu ();
        this.Children.Add (sendPage);
        this.Children.Add (livePage);
        this.Children.Add (inboxPage);
        this.Children.Add (invitePage);
    }
}
```

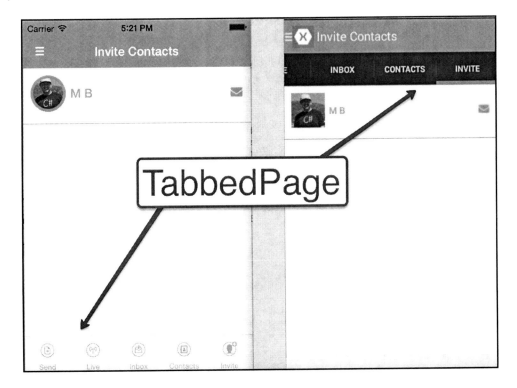

In order to work properly with `TabbedPage`, it is mandatory to give a value to the `Title` property of each content page. We can also assign the `Icon` property if we want to show it. The `Icon` property is only used by default in the iOS version of the app:

```
public SendPageMenu ()
    {
        Title = "Send";
        Icon = Icon = "menu_send.png";
    }
```

CarouselPage

`CarouselPage` displays an array of pages, each of which loads content onto the screen and allows the final user to swipe from side to side to navigate between them.

The use of it is exactly like `TabbedPage`, with the only difference being that we need to inherit from `CarouselPage`. Like we did for `TabbedPage`, we need to prepare the content pages to add to `CarouselPage`.

When we have them, we can add a new C# file called, for example, `CarouselRootPage`, and inherit from `CarouselPage`. On the constructor we can now add the pages we want to the `Children` property, and they will be reachable by the user by just swiping between pages:

```
public class CarouselRootPage : CarouselPage
{
    public CarouselRootPage  ()
    {
        SendPageMenu sendPage = new SendPageMenu();
        LivePageMenu livePage = new LivePageMenu ();
        InboxPageMenu inboxPage = new InboxPageMenu ();
        InvitePageMenu invitePage = new InvitePageMenu ();
        this.Children.Add (sendPage);
        this.Children.Add (livePage);
        this.Children.Add (inboxPage);
        this.Children.Add (invitePage);
    }
}
```

Also, in this case it is mandatory to give a value to the Title property of each content page.

> When embedding a `CarouselPage` into a `MasterDetailPage.Detail` application, we should set `MasterDetailPage.IsGestureEnabled` to `false` to prevent gesture conflicts between the `CarouselPage` and `MasterDetailPage`.

Layouts

`Xamarin.Forms` Layouts are used to compose user interface controls into logical structures. Technically, a Layout is a specialized subtype of View that acts as a container for other Layouts or Views. It contains logic to set the position and size of the child elements in `Xamarin.Forms` applications.

We will now explore all the types of layouts that are available for `Xamarin.Forms`.

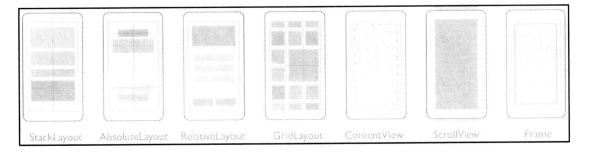

StackLayout

We can use StackLayout when we need to position elements in a single horizontal or vertical line.

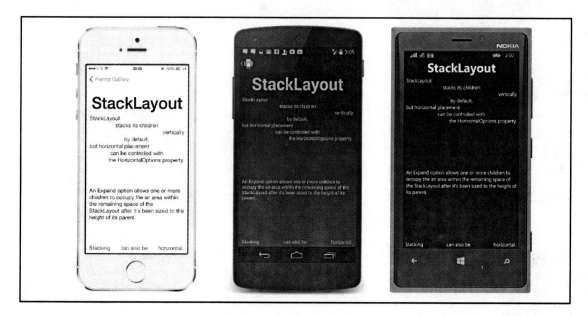

The height and width of the items placed into the layout are adjusted by the layout automatically, but if we want to we can force it using the `HeightRequest` and `WidthRequest` properties.

We can set the `Orientation` property to `StackOrientation.Horizontal` or `StackOrientation.Vertical` to sort the elements in our layout.

If we want to define a layout like this:

We can see that it is composed of two horizontal layouts.

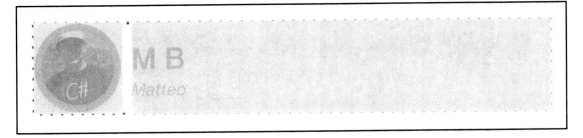

In the second layout, we can recognize two vertical layouts:

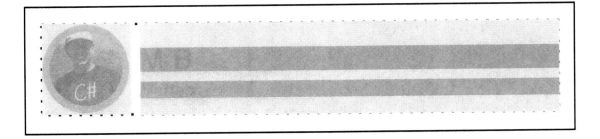

We then need to develop a stack layout structure that will appear like this:

The elements inside each single layout can be set using the `Children` property.

We can also set the distance between the border of the parent layout and the stack layout that we are building by setting the `Padding` property.

The distance between horizontal and vertical layouts can be set using the `Spacing` property:

```
StackLayout horizontalLayout = new StackLayout () {
    Orientation = StackOrientation.Horizontal,
    HeightRequest = 50,
    Spacing = 5,
    Padding = 10,
    Children = {
        image,
        new StackLayout {
            Orientation = StackOrientation.Vertical,
            Spacing = 5,
            Children = { title, subtitle }
        }
    }

};
```

StackLayout is a View, and when ready, it can add the StackLayout to the `Children` property of a page or to the `View` property of a cell.

We can also assign the `LayoutOptions` property in order to position the elements on the screen.

LayoutOptions

Views in `Xamarin.Forms` have two layout properties: `HorizontalOptions` and `VerticalOptions`. Both properties are a type of `LayoutOptions` enum.

The following are the layout options available in `Xamarin.Forms`:

- `Start`: `Start` and `StartAndExpand` position the elements at the beginning of the page
- `Center`: `Center` and `CenterAndExpand` position the elements at the center of the page
- `End`: `End` and `EndAndExpand` position the elements at the end of the page
- `Fill`: `Fill` and `FillAndExpand` position the elements from the beginning to the end of the page

Basically, the `Start`, `Center`, `End`, and `Fill` options define a view's alignment onscreen. The Expand suffix defines if a view may have more space available.

Views with the `Start`, `Center`, `End`, and `Fill` layout options preserve only a combined size of thier children.

The `Expand` suffix demands all the width or height of a screen if the view can expand and the area is available.

AbsoluteLayout

We can use AbsoluteLayout to position elements providing proportional coordinates and/or device coordinates in order to place them at absolute positions. With Absolute Layout we can position elements onscreen by aligning them to proportions. For example, we can position the Label element to half the width from the left (center) and a full height from the top (bottom) of the screen.

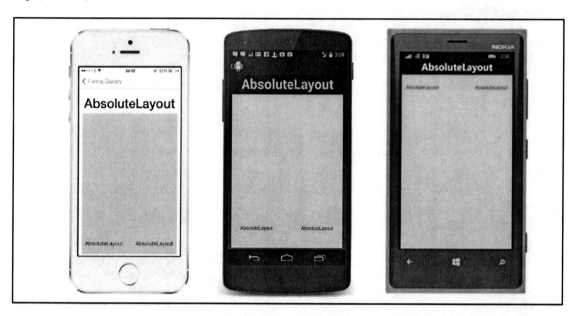

Different platforms have unique characteristics to draw a component onto the screen. For example, iOS draws tab handles on the bottom of the screen and Android draws at the top by default. Xamarin respects all platforms' unique characteristics and behaves differently on each platform. As we can see in the preceding image, the AbsoluteLayout element draws its child elements differently on each platform.

To position the element where we want, we can use AbsoluteLayoutFlags.

AbsoluteLayoutFlags is an enumerator that can have the following values:

- None
- XProportional
- YProportional
- PositionProportional
- WidthProportional
- HeigthProportional
- SizeProportional
- All

To set `AbsoluteLayoutFlags` we can use the static `SetLayoutFlags` method of `AbsoluteLayout`:

```
AbsoluteLayout.SetLayoutFlags ( child, flags );
```

We have different ways to position the children in an absolute layout.

In this example, we position the element in the left half of the layout:

```
var layout = new AbsoluteLayout();
var leftHalfOfLayoutChild = new BoxView { Color = Color.Red };
layout.Children.Add
(
    leftHalfOfLayoutChild,
    new Rectangle(0, 0, 0.5, 1),
    AbsoluteLayoutFlags.All
);
```

As we can see in the following image, we can position and scale the red box to fill the left half of the screen:

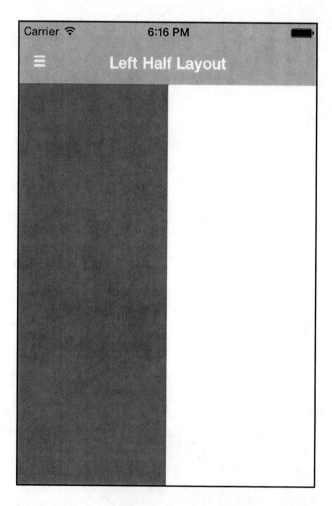

If we want to center the element and give it an automatic size, we can write it like in this example:

```
var layout = new AbsoluteLayout();
var centerAutomaticallySizedChild = new BoxView { Color = Color.Green };
layout.Children.Add
(
  centerAutomaticallySizedChild,
  new Rectangle (
  0.5,
  0.5,
```

```
    AbsoluteLayout.AutoSize,
    AbsoluteLayout.AutoSize ),
    AbsoluteLayoutFlags.PositionProportional
);
```

It will look like this:

If we don't set any flag when we define the rectangle, it will be positioned in the absolute coordinates.

RelativeLayout

In RelativeLayout, we can position elements by providing the initial coordinates and the height and width of each of them.

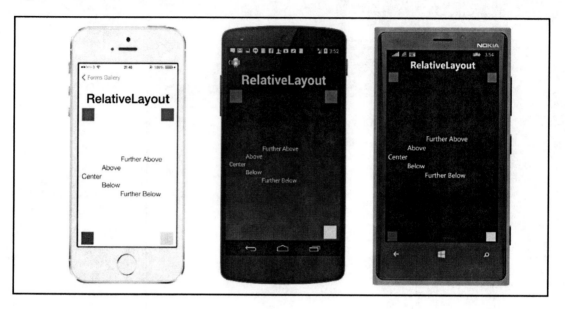

We can use the following lambda expression:

```
Constraint.RelativeToParent ((parent) => { return parent.Height / 2; }))
```

We can position an element relative to the center of its parent, as shown in the previous code.

We can do the same with the horizontal position using the Width property of the parent.

In this example, we are adding our element to the layout and positioning it horizontally in a third of the parent, Width, and vertically in half of the parent, Height:

```
relativeLayout.Children.Add (myElement,
            Constraint.RelativeToParent ((parent) => {
                return parent.Width / 3;
            }),
            Constraint.RelativeToParent ((parent) => {
                return parent.Height / 2;
            }));
```

We may use `relativeLayout` to create a screen with a background image or screen with stacked elements. As we can see in the following code, we'll have stacked boxviews:

```
relativeLayout.Children.Add (
  new BoxView() { Color = Color.Red, WidthRequest = 50, HeightRequest
  = 50 },
  Constraint.Constant (50),
  Constraint.Constant (50),
  Constraint.Constant (100),
  Constraint.Constant (100)
);

relativeLayout.Children.Add (
  new BoxView() { Color = Color.Yellow, WidthRequest = 50, HeightRequest =
50 },
  Constraint.Constant (50),
  Constraint.Constant (150),
  Constraint.Constant (100),
  Constraint.Constant (100)
);
```

Grid

The grid allows us to position elements in rows and columns.

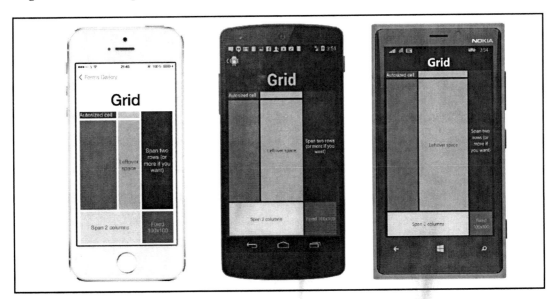

In this case, when we add an element to the `Children` property of the grid, we can define the number of the row and column where we want to put the element.

The Grid has the following properties that we can use to define our layout:

- `Children`: This is an array of elements that display in a defined position of the grid
- `ColumnDefinitions`: This allows us to set the Width of the columns
- `ColumnSpacing`: We can use this property to set the distance between columns
- `RowDefinitions`: This allows us to set the Height of the rows
- `RowSpacing`: We can use this property to set the distance between rows

For example:

```
var grid = new Grid {
    RowSpacing = 50,
    ColumnSpacing = 10
};

for (int i = 0; i < 12; i++) {
    int row = i / 3;
    int column = i % 3;

    grid.Children.Add (
    new Label {
        Text= i.ToString(),
        BackgroundColor = Color.Green
        },
    column,
    row);
}
```

The result of this code will be something like this:

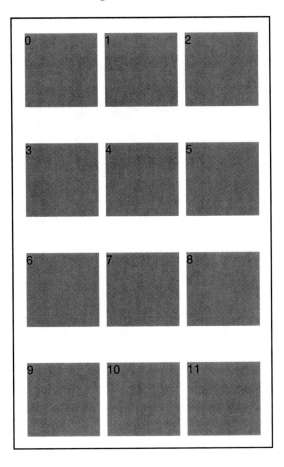

ContentView

ContentView is useful when we need a placeholder that contains a single child element.

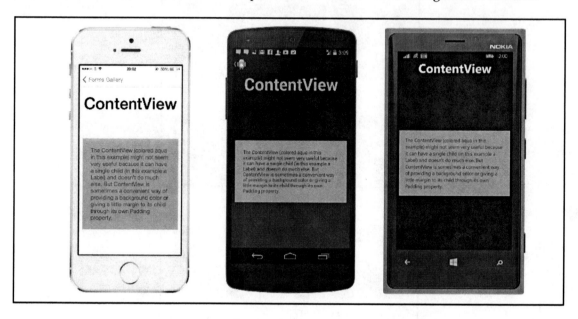

This is probably the simplest layout we can imagine in `Xamarin.Forms`.

In this case, we only have the availability of the `Content` property, and we can set it with just one Element. This is typically used as root for other customized layouts.

For example:

```
var layout = new ContentView {
    Content = new Label { Text = "I'm Content!" },
};
```

ScrollView

ScrollView is very useful when we need to have scrollable content.

We can set one single element using the `Content` property, and we can also set the Orientation property in order to indicate the scroll direction (horizontal or vertical).

For example:

```
StackLayout stack = new StackLayout();
for (var i=0; i<100; i++)
{
    stack.Children.Add (
      new Button {
        Text = i.ToString()
      }
    );
}

ScrollView scrollview = new ScrollView {
 Content = stack
};
```

The result of this code will be a scrollable list of 100 labels.

```
35

36

37

38

39

40

41

42

43

44

45

46
```

ScrollView may be used to create a scrollable list, but in terms of memory management and performance, it's better to use native lists. Each platform has its own list component to stack elements. These components provide more control over list items, provide better CPU and RAM usage, and better customization. We should always consider using native list elements instead of ScrollView.

Frame

We can use Frame when we need to embed a single element and give it a container with a shadow or outline border.

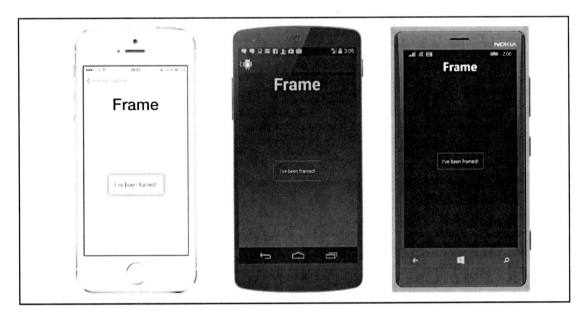

In a Frame layout we can set the `HasShadow` property to true or false to either add or not add a shadow to the container, and we can set the `OutlineColor` property to specify the color assigned to the border.

For example:

```
var frame = new Frame {
    Content = new Label { Text = "I <3 Xamarin.Forms" },
    OutlineColor = Color.Silver,
    HasShadow = true
};
```

This example produces the following layout:

Views

Xamarin.Forms Views are the building blocks of cross-platform mobile user interfaces. They are visual objects such as buttons, labels, and text entry boxes. These UI elements are typically subclasses of View.

ActivityIndicator

ActivityIndicator is a visual control used to indicate that something is ongoing. This control gives a visual clue to the user that something is happening, without including information about its progress.

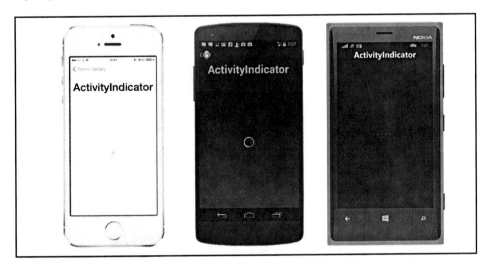

This component is very useful for notifying the user when we need to do some asynchronous work that takes time.

To do so, we can implement the `INotifyPropertyChanged` interface in our service or data class and add a Boolean property that we will call `IsLoading`:

```
private bool isLoading;

        public bool IsLoading {
            get { return isLoading; }
            set {
                isLoading = value;
                if (PropertyChanged != null)
                    PropertyChanged ();
            }
        }

        #region INotifyPropertyChanged implementation

        public event PropertyChangedEventHandler PropertyChanged;

        #endregion
```

We can use this property to notify users when we are loading data and when we have finished.

The last step is to bind this property with the visibility of the `ActivityIndicator`:

```
ActivityIndicator activityIndicator = new ActivityIndicator ();
activityIndicator.SetBinding (ActivityIndicator.IsVisibleProperty,
"IsLoading");
activityIndicator.SetBinding (ActivityIndicator.IsRunningProperty,
"IsLoading");
```

BoxView

We can use the BoxView to draw a solid colored rectangle.

The box is a simple component.

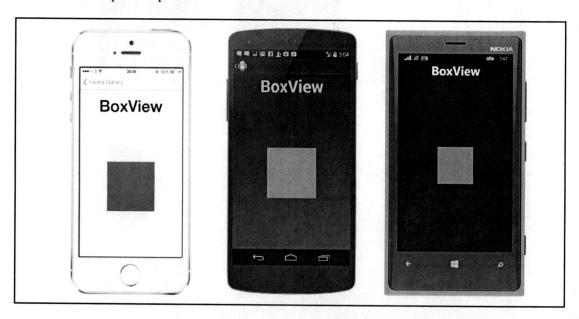

We can define the color of it and we can position it in a layout:

```
var box = new BoxView { Color = Color.Blue };
```

Button

The element button reacts to touch events. We can manage and handle our actions with the touch event.

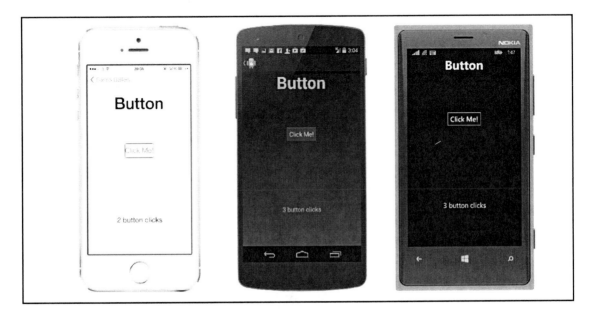

DatePicker

DatePicker is an element that allows the user to input a date with a scrollable interface.

Editor

We can use this control when we need the user to edit multiple lines of text.

Entry

We can use this control when we need the user to edit a single line of text.

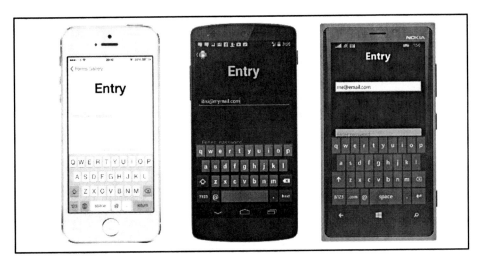

Image

We can use this element to add an image.

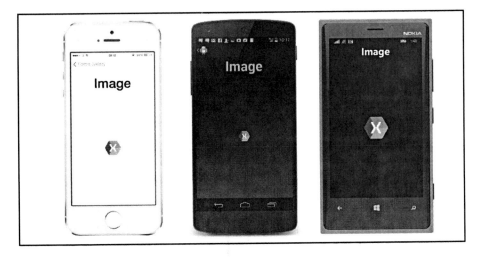

Label

The label is a very common and basic element that we can use to display text.

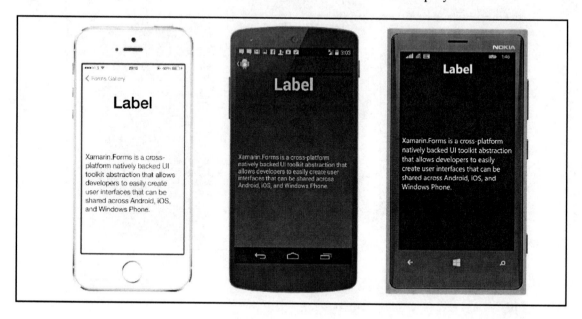

ListView

We can use the ListView control to display scrolling lists of data.

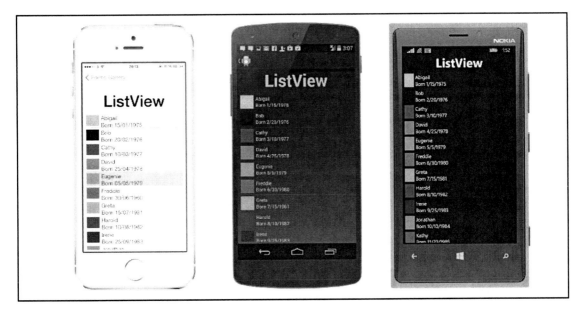

In order to develop a ListView, we need to first define three classes:

- `Item`: The raw description of the single element to display
- `Data`: The list of items with all the data to display
- `Cell`: The layout of the single element to display

When we have those three classes we can use them together in our ListView.

In our example, we want to display a list of items with a coloured box, a name, and a birthdate.

First, we create a new class called `MyItem` and add three properties: `BoxColor`, `Name`, and `Birthdate`:

```
public class MyItem
    {
        public Color BoxColor {
            get;
            set;
        }

        public string Name {
            get;
            set;
        }

        public DateTime Birthdate {
            get;
            set;
        }
    }
```

Now we need to create the `MyItemData` class, which will be a list of `MyItem` and will contain all the data that we need to display:

```
public class MyItemData : List<MyItem>
{
  public MyItemData ()
  {
    this.Add (new MyItem {
    Name = "Engin",
    Birthdate = DateTime.Parse ("20/10/1979"),
    BoxColor = Color.Blue
    });
    //... add all the items or load them from a db
  }
}
```

The last step we need to follow before creating the ListView is to create the ViewCell. So, now we will create a new class called `MyItemCell`, which needs to inherit from ViewCell.

Here, we will define the layout for the single cell.

We have to define a box and set the binding of the `BackgroundColor` property to `BoxColor` and the two labels setting the binding of the `Text` property to `Name` and `Birthdate`.

After that, we can compose our layout, as we've seen in the layout section of this chapter:

```
public class MyItemCell : ViewCell
{
    public MyItemCell ()
    {
        BoxView box = new BoxView ();
        box.SetBinding (VisualElement.BackgroundColorProperty,
        new Binding ("BoxColor"));

        Label nameLabel = new Label ();
        nameLabel.SetBinding (Label.TextProperty,
        new Binding ("Name"));

        Label birthDateLabel = new Label ();
        birthDateLabel.SetValue (Label.TextProperty,
        new Binding ("BirthDate"));

        View =    new StackLayout {
            Orientation = StackOrientation.Horizontal,
            Children = {
                box,
                new StackLayout {
                    Orientation = StackOrientation.Vertical,
                    Children = { nameLabel, birthDateLabel }
                }
            }
        };
    }
}
```

We are now ready to create our ListView. We can create a new file called `MyListView` and add this code on the constructor:

```
public class MyListView : ListView
{
    public MyListView ()
    {
        List<MyItem> data = new List<MyItem> ();
        ItemsSource = data;
        DataTemplate cell = new DataTemplate (typeof(MyItemCell));
        ItemTemplate = cell;

        //additional properties
        VerticalOptions = LayoutOptions.Fill;
        BackgroundColor = Color.Transparent;
        HasUnevenRows = true;
        SelectedItem = null;
```

```
            IsPullToRefreshEnabled = true;
            SeparatorVisibility = SeparatorVisibility.None;
        }
    }
```

We first define the data and assign it to the `ItemsSource` property of ListView.

Then, we just need to define ItemTemplate; we can use the custom cell we've already created.

We also have the option to define other properties:

- `VerticalOption`: How to fill the space vertically in the container with the ListView
- `BackgroundColor`: The background color of our ListView
- `HasUnevenRow`: If we assign this property as true, we can define a custom height for each cell
- `SelectedItem`: Here, we can decide to show one item as selected, or we can set it to null if we want all the items to be unselected
- `IsPullToRefreshEnabled`: When true, it automatically enables the `PullToRefresh` function to refresh the data in ListView
- `SeparatorVisibility`: We can set this property as `Default` or `None` to show or hide a separator between the items
- `SeparatorColor`: Here, we can define the color of the separator line

OpenGLView

When we need to add OpenGL content to our app, we can use the OpenGLView element. OpenGL is currently supported on iOS and Android; Windows alternatively supports DirectX. Both OpenGL and DirectX are core frameworks optimized for game development. OpenGLView is for displaying OpenGL content (such as part of a game) where we want onscreen.

Picker

This control offers the user the possibility to pick an element in a list.

ProgressBar

We can use the `ProgressBar` control when we want to display the progress of some activity in our app.

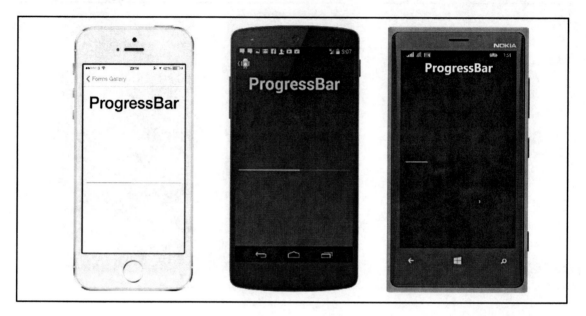

SearchBar

This element provides a search box. SearchBar in Xamarin.Forms has several properties to implement a good search experience:

- `Placeholder`: Default text, shown to the user when SearchBar is empty
- `Text`: Default text will appear inside of SearchBar
- `CancelButtonColor`: Specifies the foreground text color of Cancel button
- `SearchCommand`: Actual binding method that executes search logic
- `SearchCommandParameter`: Extra parameter for the search command

We may create an exact result with both the Entry view and Button view. However, it takes extra development and **SearchBar** already has it. It's good practice to try not to reinvent the wheel.

Slider

When we want the user to input a linear value, the slider is the element for us.

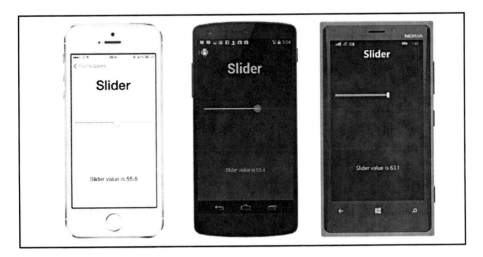

Stepper

We can use this element when we need the user to input a discrete value constrained to a range.

Switch

The switch is an element that provides a toggled value.

TableView

TableView has a behavior similar to ListView.

The difference is that we can use TableView as a container to build up data input and display forms using different cell types.

TableView does not support data-binding, so we must add rows dynamically to its Children collection.

TimePicker

TimePicker is an element that allows the user to input a time with a scrollable interface.

WebView

The WebView control allows users to browse websites or HTML generated in code.

Although the best solution for showing an entire website from the app is to redirect the user to the specific browser, we can use WebView to present a HTML page embedded in our app. If we want to, we can also build our own embedded web browser.

When we embed a WebView on Xamarin.Forms, it uses the native web browser control on each platform.

Local resources can also be displayed.

To display a web page by loading a URL from the Internet, we just need to set the Source property on the WebView control.

Cells

We already mentioned cells when we talked about the ListView element. Cells can be added to ListViews and TableViews. It is a specialized element used for items in a table and describes how each item in a list should be drawn.

Cell describes a template for creating a visual element.

In Xamarin.Forms, we can develop our own custom cells, but we also have the availability of defined cells:

- `EntryCell`: A cell with a label and a single line text entry field
- `SwitchCell`: A cell with a label and an on/off switch

- `TextCell`: A cell with primary text and detail text
- `ImageCell`: A cell that has an image

Pop-ups

We can use two pop-up-like user interface elements: alert or action sheet.

For interacting with the user via a pop-up, we can use two methods in the Page class: DisplayAlert and DisplayActionSheet.

They are rendered with the appropriate native controls on each platform.

Gestures

Code can react to taps on most user interface objects in Xamarin.Forms.

We can use the Xamarin.Forms GestureRecognizer class for tap detection on user interface controls.

The number of taps can be specified to produce double-tap (or triple-tap or more) behavior.

To make an image clickable, we need to:

- Create a `TapGestureRecognizer` instance
- Handle the tapped event
- Add the new gesture recognizer to the `GestureRecognizers` collection on the image

```
<Image Source="switch-off.jpg">
    <Image.GestureRecognizers>
        <TapGestureRecognizer
                Tapped="OnTapGestureRecognizerTapped"
                NumberOfTapsRequired="2" />
    </Image.GestureRecognizers>
</Image>
```

GestureRecognizer **usage inside of an** Image **element with Xaml.**

```
void OnTapGestureRecognizerTapped(object sender, EventArgs args) {
    tapCount++;
    var imageSender = (Image)sender;
```

```
    if (tapCount % 2 == 0) {
        imageSender.Source = "switch-off.jpg";
    } else {
        imageSender.Source = "switch-on.jpg";
    }
}
```

The code for the event handler (in the example) increments a counter and changes the image from `switch-off.jpg` to `switch-on.jpg`.

We can also make a UI element draggable with a pan gesture, as shown in the following code. This time we won't use Xaml and will instead use `PanGestureRecognizer` via code.

 Creating pages with Xaml is called Declarative Programming, and creating pages with code is called Imperative Programming. Generally speaking, Declarative Programming usually makes coding more readable, understandable, and scalable. Imperative Programming requires the developer to code the desired behavior step by step.

```
var panGesture = new PanGestureRecognizer();
panGesture.PanUpdated += (s, e) => {
  // Handle the pan
};
image.GestureRecognizers.Add(panGesture);
```

 Xamarin.Forms has a GestureRecognizer class to detect Tap, Pan, and Pinch gestures on UI elements. If we need to support custom gestures (such as Rotate, Two Finger Tap, and so on), we may create a class, implement the IGestureRecognizer interface and code the desired gesture detection algorithm.

Fonts

Font information can be specified in code or in Xaml. It is also possible to use a custom font. For setting a font in code, use the three font-related properties of any controls that display text:

- `FontFamily`: The string font name
- `FontSize`: The font size as a double
- `FontAttributes`: A string specifying style information such as Italic and Bold (using the `FontAttributes` enumeration in C#).

Colors

Xamarin.Forms provides a flexible cross-platform `Color` class.

The `Color` class provides a number of methods for building a color instance.

We can use a collection of common colors, including Red, Green, and Blue but we also have other ways of making our own color:

- `FromHex`: A string value similar to the syntax used in HTML, for example, `00FF00`. Alpha can optionally be specified as the first pair of characters (`CC00FF00`).
- `FromHsla`: Hue, saturation, and luminosity double values, with an optional alpha value (0.0-1.0)
- `FromRgb`: Red, green, and blue int values (0-255)
- `FromRgba`: Red, green, blue, and alpha int values (0-255)
- `FromUint`: Sets a single double value representing argb

Summary

In this chapter we learned about rendering models, the Application class and its importance, different page types (such as Content, Master-Detail, Navigation, and so on), Layout types (such as Stack, Absolute, Grid, and so on), and Views (such as DatePicker, ProgressBar, Slider, and so on).

Now we're ready to move on to the next chapter, where we'll learn how to properly structure our solution. We'll also learn about the Presentation, Business, and Data layers, as well as how to develop base models of these layers.

4
Data – the Monkeys Catalog

We have started this book sitting in a virtual airplane that is now flying us over Xamarin Mobile Multiplatform Development. It's time to look down a little bit and view the map of the land that we are going to visit every time we make a new app.

One common thing about each app that we develop is that, at some point, we will need to write and read data.

Unfortunately, when we work with mobile phones we cannot trust the network and we cannot have a full-time communication with a central SQL server. This means that we need to find a way to save data locally and then synchronize it with the server as soon as we've got connectivity.

In this chapter, we will explore how to design and develop an architecture that allows us to work with and manage local data.

Mobile architectural pattern

When we start to design a new app we should group the core functionality in logical components. These logical groupings are called layers. Layers help to differentiate between the different kinds of task performed by the components, making the reusability and maintenance of our code easier. Each logical layer contains a number of discrete component types grouped into sub-layers, with each sub-layer performing a specific type of task.

Having an application divided into separate layers, each one of them has distinct roles and functionality that help us with the following:

- Maximizing maintainability of the code
- Answering "Where should I create this file?" or "Where should I install this package?"
- Optimizing the way that the application works when deployed in different ways and sharing most of the backend logic between platforms

Presentation, business, and data layers

We can imagine our app as a set of cooperating components grouped into layers.

A simplified representation of how we need to structure our app shows the high-level layers and their relationships with users and other applications and services:

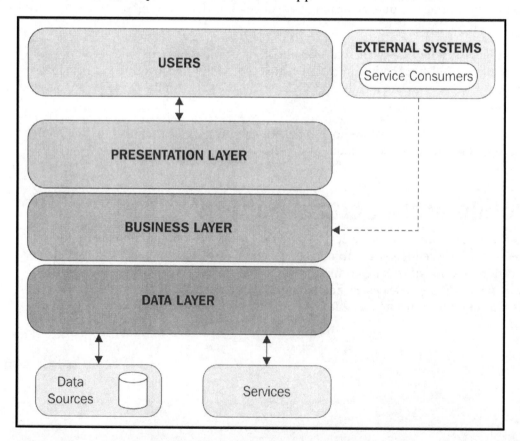

This is a basic principle in software development and usually it is a good practice to create a different library (a new project) for each of those layers. When we develop mobile applications we need to balance the number of libraries with the limited performance of a mobile device.

In order to have a nice structure of our code, well balanced with the performances, we can create folders inside our project instead of multiple projects.

We can start creating a folder called `Base` and a folder called `Core` inside the main Xamarin Form project.

We are going to explore how to design and create our objects and functionality to manage the core of the entire app. Let's have a quick overview of the layers that we are going to create as folders and the meaning we will give to them:

- `Presentation Layer`: In this folder, we will insert the User-Oriented functionality responsible for managing user interaction with our app. Those components provide a bridge into the core business logic that we will create on the business layer.
- `Business Layer`: In this folder, we will implement the core functionality of our system.

  The business logic is the way we will have to call one or more data components or services interfaces. It should be the only access point for the presentation layer to our core.

- `Data Layer`: Here we will implement the access to the data that is embedded in our system or exposed from other networked systems. The business layer consumes the objects in the data layer.

  It would be very useful to build our helpers in order to minimize the code to write, in order to make our data component.

- `Services`: A service is a way to communicate with other systems by passing messages. It can be considered from our app as a component, but in reality, if we explore it, we will discover that it is a software component like any other, a system that in general can be logically grouped into presentation, business, and data layers, like any other application.

  Our app can make use of the services without being aware of the way they are implemented, but accessing them using their presentation layer, just like our final user will be able to use our app without being aware of this book and our architecture strategies.

- `Service Layer`: This is an optional layer that we might consider to add to our app when we decide to provide services to other apps.

  In this case, we can expose the business functionality as services providing a new channel to access the application.

Inside the layers

We are going to create inside each folder the core of our app, which includes data management. We want to build an example of a catalog that will be platform independent. The catalog will contain our data and needs to be easy to manage and maintain in the future.

Before starting the fun part of writing code, we will have an overview of the best practices and patterns that are going to help us to reach our goals. For those of us who are moving from developing servers or web solutions to mobile development, one of the first questions might be "How can I connect my database to a mobile app?"

We will find an answer to this very soon.

A mobile app, compared with server and web solutions, has the great advantage that it is a system used by an individual user. Sometimes we need to store and read data that needs to be synchronized with a central server. A central server can communicate with other systems using the Internet network.

In a mobile environment, we cannot trust on the network availability. For this reason, we need to have a way to store data locally on the mobile phone and to synchronize it as soon as we have an available network.

In this chapter, we are focusing on the local data, but we will soon create in this book a Mobile Support Infrastructure that allows the central server to provide our mobile app a channel of communication with the central database.

We now need to understand how to design and develop a base library that will help us to speed up our development and maintenance.

Here is a map that will help us to remember the structure of our solution:

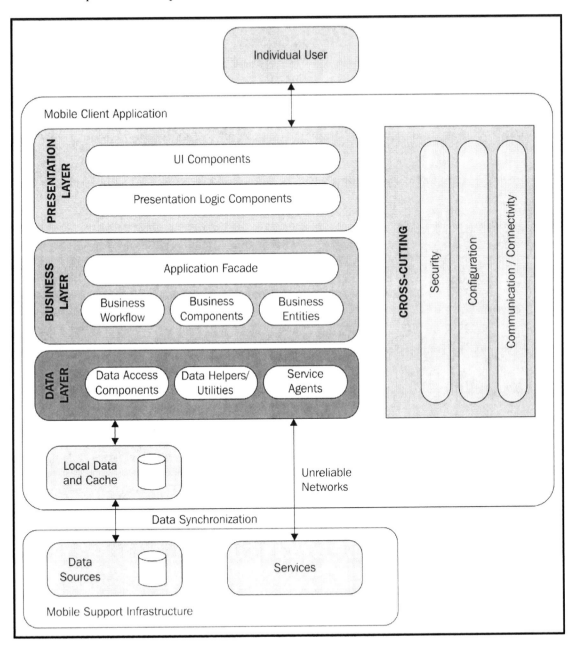

The Monkeys catalog

We can now create a new solution.

On the New Project Pad, we have to select Mobile Apps and Blank App (Xamarin Forms Portable).

We can give it the name `XamarinByExample.MonkeysCatalogue` and then click on **OK**.

Xamarin Studio will create the template for us with the PCL project and the platform-specific projects.

We can now prepare the architectural folders.

Let's add in the root of the project, `XamarinByExample.MonkeysCatalogue`, the `base` and `core` folders.

Base folders

It is a good practice to create base classes as the backbone for our architecture. We will see the benefit of that every time we need to add or modify some common functionality that our core might need.

To separate the base classes from our custom solution we will add the Data, Business, Presentation, and Services folders, where we can create the Base objects for each layer.

Before we continue, we need to import the SQLite.Net PCL package from NuGet. NuGet is a space where we can find a lot of additional libraries that we can use in our apps.

To add the SQLite.Net component we need to double-click on the packages folder and write `SQLite.Net PCL` in the search box of the NuGet Pad.

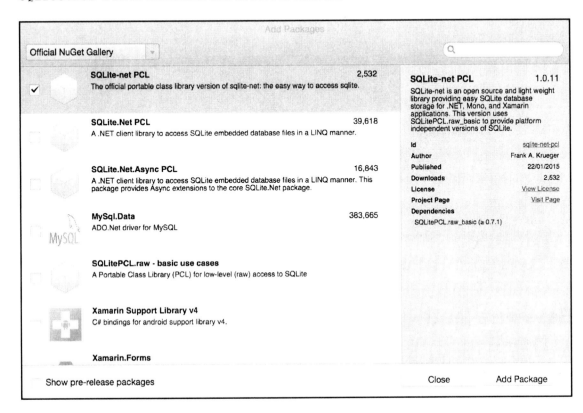

Now we can select SQLite.Net PCL, which provides us with the classes to manage an SQLite database.

In the same way, we also need to add the same package to the platform-specific project.

Base entities

The tables in our code are represented by entities.

The entities are classes that contain just the properties necessary for the description of the objects we need. One example of a base entity might be an empty object with a primary key. Each table needs a primary key. The idea of adding it to the base class allows us to forget about it every time we inherit from the base class.

What we need to do is create a class called `BaseEntity`, and add a property called `Key`:

```
using SQLite.Net.Attributes;

namespace XamarinByExample.MonkeysCatalogue
{
    public class BaseEntity<TKey>
    {
        [PrimaryKey]
        public TKey Key {
            get;
            set;
        }
    }
}
```

The `TKey` type is a generic type that we will specify when we'll create the specific classes. We will define it as the specific type (such as string or int) that we want our primary key to be. We will use generics types again in our base libraries.

Generics allow us to have more flexibility when we develop our custom objects.

Base data layer

The SQLite library we've imported from NuGet provides the helpers we need to communicate with the database.

We can focus on developing the BaseData in order to provide our core components with a tool that allows us to write as little as possible.

Let's create a class called `BaseData` in the `Data` folder.

We will use two generics types here: `TEntity` and `TKey`.

We now can define two constraints for the `TEntity` type:

- `TEntity` needs to be a `BaseEntity`

- `TEntity` needs to have an empty constructor

These constraints allow us to use `TEntity` as a `BaseEntity` and to define an instance of it when we need it inside our `BaseData`:

```
public class BaseData<TEntity, TKey>
    where TEntity : BaseEntity<TKey>, new()
```

We now need a property that contains the local database connection:

```
public SQLiteConnection DatabaseConnection {
  get;
  set;
}
```

To open a database connection, we need to know the complete database path.

We can create a `Configuration` class in the Base folder in order to save this information as well as other configuration information that we might need in the future.

We define it as partial because we might need to add some platform-specific configuration in the future:

```
public static partial class Configuration
{
    private static string _databasePath;

    public static string DatabasePath {
        get {
            if (string.IsNullOrEmpty(_databasePath)) {
                _databasePath = "monkey.db";
            }
            return _databasePath; }
        set { _databasePath = value; }
    }
}
```

We will use static variables for this information because we want to share it to all the instances of our classes.

Ways to read and write files are different on each platform. For this reason, we need to apply a small fix before we start the app in Android.

On the `MainActivity` of the Android project, before the `LoadApplication` call, we need to set the right path for the database.

We don't need to do that for other platforms:

```
var path = System.Environment.GetFolderPath
(System.Environment.SpecialFolder.ApplicationData);
if (!System.IO.Directory.Exists (path)) {
    System.IO.Directory.CreateDirectory (path);
}

var filename = Path.Combine (path, "monkey.db");
```

```
if (!System.IO.File.Exists(filename)) {
    System.IO.File.Create (filename);
}
//Set a new value for the Configuration
Configuration.DatabasePath = filename;
```

We are now ready to create the constructors of our BaseData.

We want to have an empty constructor, and a constructor that takes an existing SQL connection as a parameter.

We can start from the one that needs the SQLiteConnection as input.

Inside the constructor we want to assign a value to our `DatabaseConnection` property and we want to create a table that is able to contain our entity when this table doesn't already exist.

The `CreateTable` method of `DatabaseConnection` does it:

```
public BaseData (SQLiteConnection databaseConnection)
{
    DatabaseConnection = databaseConnection;
    DatabaseConnection.CreateTable<TEntity> (CreateFlags.AllImplicit);
}
```

In the empty constructor, we can call the other constructor using the statement `this` after the declaration, and create a new instance of the SQLiteConnection by using the database path that we've saved in our configuration class:

```
public BaseData () :
  this (new SQLiteConnection (Configuration.DatabasePath))
{
}
```

The minimum set of methods that we expect to have in a DataLayer class is called CRUD, which means Create, Read, Update, and Delete.

Create

We can add a method called Create that accepts an item of the `TEntity` type as input.

`DatabaseConnection` contains a method to insert an item in a specific table.

This makes our base method really easy to implement:

```
public void Create (TEntity item)
{
    DatabaseConnection.Insert (item, typeof(TEntity));
}
```

Read

The Read method, in general, needs to have a list of all the items saved in the table or a specific item that has something that we can query as a primary key.

We will create two overloads of the Read method.

An overload is the ability to create multiple methods of the same name with different implementations.

The first overload takes the key as an input and uses the Get method of DatabaseConnection in order to retrieve the item we need:

```
public TEntity Read (TKey key)
{
    return DatabaseConnection.Get<TEntity> (key);
}
```

The second overload doesn't take anything as an input parameter and returns the complete list of items that are in the database table:

```
public List<TEntity> Read ()
{
    List<TEntity> returnItem = new List<TEntity> ();
    TableQuery<TEntity> itemList = DatabaseConnection.Table
    <TEntity>();

    for (int i = 0; i < itemList.Count (); i++) {
        returnItem.Add (itemList.ElementAt (i));
    }
    return returnItem;
}
```

Update

The base `Update` method can use the one available in the `DatabaseConnection`:

```
public void Update (TEntity item)
{
    DatabaseConnection.Update (item, typeof(TEntity));
}
```

Delete

The base `Delete` method can use the one available in the `DatabaseConnection`:

```
public void Delete (TKey key)
{
    DatabaseConnection.Delete (key);
}
```

Base business layer

The business layer has to be a bridge between the presentation layer and the data layer.

We will use generics again, as per the data layer:

```
public class BaseBusiness<TEntity,TKey>
   where TEntity : BaseEntity<TKey>, new()
```

We need to have a data component property in order to manage the way we want to save and synchronize data:

```
public BaseData<TEntity,TKey> DataComponent {
    get;
    set;
}
```

We also need a constructor that assigns a value to our `DataComponent`:

```
public BaseBusiness ( BaseData<TEntity,TKey> dataComponent )
{
    DataComponent = dataComponent;
}
```

In general, a base business layer contains the CRUD, but in this case, we might want to override the implementation of these methods in order to add some more functionality to our custom object.

Overriding methods is a feature that allows a subclass or child class (in our case, the classes that are going to inherit from our BaseBusinnes) to provide a specific implementation of a method that is already provided.

To allow the overriding we need to define our methods as virtual. Here is the implementation of our CRUD in the base business class:

```
public virtual void Create (TEntity item)
{
    DataComponent.Create (item);
}

public virtual List<TEntity> Read ()
{
    return DataComponent.Read ();
}

public virtual TEntity Read (TKey key)
{
    return DataComponent.Read (key);
}

public virtual void Update (TEntity item)
{
    DataComponent.Update (item);
}

public virtual void Delete (TKey key)
{
    DataComponent.Delete (key);
}
```

Now that we are happy enough with our base classes, we can move on to our Core implementation.

Core folder

In this folder, we are going to create the Data, Business, Presentation, and Services folders in which we can define the core objects of our app.

We need to have a local repository of our monkeys.

First think we define our entity: the monkey class.

Core entities

Let's create a new class called `monkey` as an empty C# class.

To take advantage of our base classes, we need to use the base entity on the declaration of the class. We want the Key to be an integer so we will specify the type `TKey` of the `BaseEntity` as `int`.

Our Monkey class will automatically contain a property called `Key`, which is typed as an Integer with the right attribute `[PrimaryKey]` ready for the database:

```
public class Monkey : BaseEntity<int>
```

We need to define the empty constructor calling the base constructor contained in the `BaseEntity`:

```
public Monkey () : base ()
{
}
```

Now we can just define the properties that describe our monkey class:

```
public int ScientificClassificationKey {
    get;
    set;
}

public string Name {
    get;
    set;
}

public DateTime Birthdate {
    get;
    set;
}

public char Gender {
    get;
    set;
}
```

We can now start developing the core data layer.

Core data layer

Since we've done most of the work on our base class, the only thing we need now is to inherit from it and define an empty constructor that calls the `BaseData` constructor:

```
public class MonkeyData : BaseData<Monkey,int>
{
    public MonkeyData () : base()
    {
    }
}
```

That's it!

And it will be as easy as this for each of our objects that inherit from BaseEntity J.

Core business layer

We've also done most of the work on our base class for the business layer.

We need to inherit from the BaseBusiness and define an empty constructor that calls the base constructor with the instance of the right data layer, in this case, the `MonkeyData`:

```
public class MonkeyBusiness : BaseBusiness<Monkey,int>
{
    public MonkeyBusiness () : base (new MonkeyData ())
    {
    }
}
```

If we want to do something more in the `MonkeyBusiness` class, we always have access to the `DataComponent` and we can override the CRUD. By writing override and blank space, Xamarin Studio gives us the list of the methods we can override. If we select one of them and press Enter we will have a base implementation of the method we've selected where we can write additional code:

```
1 using System;
2
3 namespace XamarinByExample.MonkeysCatalogue
4 {
5     public class MonkeyBusiness : BaseBusiness<Monkey,int>
6     {
7         public MonkeyBusiness () : base (new MonkeyData ())
8         {
9         }
10
11         override |
12     }
13 }
14
15
```

```
☐ Create(Monkey item)          public virtual void Create (
☐ Delete(int key)                  Monkey item
☐ Equals(object obj)           )
☐ GetHashCode()
☐ Read()
☐ Read(int key)
☐ ToString()
```

If we press *Enter* on the `Create` method, this code will be inserted from Xamarin Studio:

```
public override void Create (Monkey item)
{
    base.Create (item);
}
```

It is always good practice, when we override a method, to call the base implementation of it by using the base statement.

Presentation

In order to see what we've created, we can now modify the
`XamarinByExample.MonkeysCatalogue` file that contains the template written by
Xamarin studio when we created the new solution.

In the presentation layer, when we need to save or read data, we should always use the
business layer contained in our core library.

Inside the app constructor we can instantiate our `MonkeyBusiness` and insert a new
monkey in our database:

```
MonkeyBusiness targetMonkey = new MonkeyBusiness ();

Monkey monkeyToSave = new Monkey () {
    Key = 0,
    Name = "Xamarin Monkey",
    Gender = "Male",
    ScientificClassificationKey = 10,
    Birthdate = DateTime.Parse("11/11/1980")
};

targetMonkey.Create (monkeyToSave);
```

Then we can read from the database and save the result in our local variable,
`fromDatabase`:

```
Monkey fromDatabase = targetMonkey.Read (0);
```

Now we can just modify the default implementation to check the content of our
`fromDatabase` variable:

```
MainPage = new ContentPage {
    Content = new StackLayout {
        VerticalOptions = LayoutOptions.Center,
        Children = {
            new Label {
                XAlign = TextAlignment.Center,
                Text = fromDatabase.ToString()
            }
        }
    }
};
```

When we execute the code we will have these results:

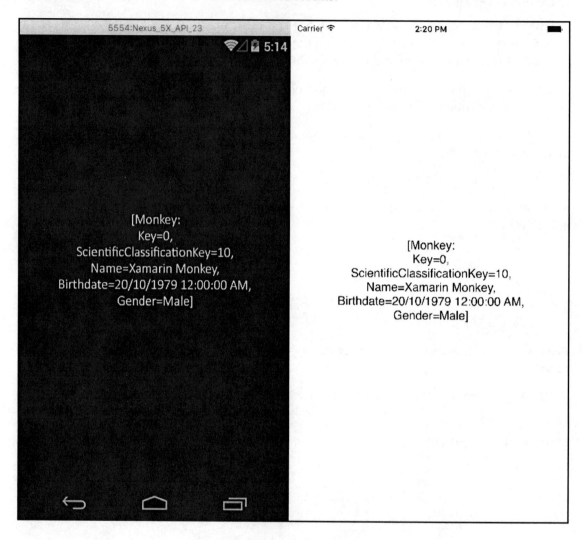

Summary

In this chapter, we've explored the best practices for a mobile software architecture. We've developed our own Base and Core architectures. We've used a NuGet package called `SQLite.Net PCL` as a helper for the operations needed to create a local storage. We've learned how generics can help when implementing and using base classes. We also used the inheritance and overload of functions and the override of base methods.

We'll examine communication models and pursue the answers of these questions in the next chapter:

- How can we make async calls over the Internet?
- How can we take advantage of cloud platforms?

We'll also dive into making requests to web services and RESTful services in the next chapter.

5
Cloud and Async Communication

In this chapter, we are going to explore how to manage the communication in our app.

We will start learning how to develop async functionality. Then we will explore the different formats of data and messages that we can use to exchange messages in a communication channel.

Our goal will be to develop examples and to be able, by the end of the chapter, to integrate our app with external services and functionalities provided by a server.

Communication

ATIS: "Xamarin International automated airport information Sierra, 0583B1. Bandwidth 280 at 10. Visibility 6 miles. Few cloud APIs at 7,000 feet. Temperature 16, Dew point 15. Altimeter 14.13. Landing and departing runway 12. Taxiway Sierra closed. Caution: developers near the airport. Inform Server City on initial contact that you have received information Sierra."

CAP: "Developer 123 Roger, Sierra received"

ATC: "Developer 123 Xamarin approach, recycle transponder, squawk 0123 and ident"

CAP: "Developer 123 Roger, ident you have"

Data, format, and channel

In real life and in computing, communication is based on data interchange.

To communicate allows us to convey a meaning through shared systems. It makes it possible to partition tasks and workloads between people and people, people and systems, and systems and systems.

A model of communication between computing systems is called a Client-Server model. A Server can be considered as a provider of resources and services. A Client is the consumer of the resources and services provided by the server. Both the Client and Server are software components that run in one or more computing devices called hosts.

Clients and Servers communicate through a channel called communication channel.

In a communication channel, messages can transit. There are many types of communication channels and there are different formats of messages.

Hardware components installed on Client and Server hosts provide access to communication channels. Mobile devices commonly support Wi-Fi, 3G, and Bluetooth.

Some devices are also enabled to other channels such as, for example, **Near Field Communication (NFC).** Communication channels enable us to build a network. When developing for mobile we cannot assume that we will always have an open communication channel. The network in a mobile context is not reliable and we need to consider that when designing and developing a solution.

Sync and async communication

Before we start coding, we will have an overview of what synchronous and asynchronous contexts are, what are the differences, and when and how to develop a sync or an async backend in order to manage communications in our apps.

Imagine a real-life situation where we are in a fast food restaurant and we need to place our order. Our user experience expectation is pretty simple:

1. Wait for the availability of the fast food attendant.
2. Order two items from the menu (a sandwich and a soft drink).
3. Pay.
4. Wait for the food.
5. Sit on a table to eat or take away the items.

The fast food counter will be our user interface and the fast food attendant will be our application interface. Everything that happens behind the counter will represent the backend and will be managed by the fast food attendant under our requests.

In a synchronous context, the fast food attendant will ask us to place our orders one at a time and will also ask us to wait until the placed order is ready to be dispatched. Only then will we be able to place another order. For example, when we ask for a sandwich, the fast food attendant starts to make it and doesn't listen to any other requests. They will be available to listen to the next request (we also want a soft drink) only when they have delivered the sandwich to us.

This approach will lock any requests from us or from other people that are in the queue until each single result for each single request has been provided.

In an asynchronous context, the main fast food attendant will always be available to listen to the requests from the customers and will pass those requests to other people behind the fast food counter.

From now on, we will call the main fast food attendant the **Main Thread**. The Main Thread will be the only one able to accept requests and deliver results from and to the customers. The fast food counter is the user interface and only the Main Thread will be able to update its status.

We will give the name **Secondary Threads** to the people available to perform other tasks requested by the Main Thread.

When one of the pending requests made by the Main Thread is ready to be presented, the Secondary Thread raises an alert with the result of the job. This alert is called **Event** and the Main Thread listens to these Events, subscribing them and managing them in one method called the **Event Handler.** The sandwich is ready; the main fast food attendant receives it from a secondary attendant and can now deliver it to the customer.

The advantage of this approach is that, as customers (users), our perception of the system will be improved by the fact that it became more responsive. We have to consider that more responsive doesn't mean faster. If our sandwich requires five minutes to prepare, it will still be ready in five minutes. The real advantage for us is that at the same time we can start enjoying our soft drink while waiting.

We can now translate this real-life story to a cross-platform app.

Example project – Xamarin Fast Food

First of all, we can create a new Xamarin.Forms PCL project and reuse the same base structure that we created in Chapter 4, *Data – the Monkeys Catalog*.

We can copy all the classes we've written inside the Base folder and we can prepare the empty subfolders of Core to define the business logic of our project.

To use the Base classes, we need to import into our projects the SQLite.Net PCL from the NuGet Package manager. It is a good practice to update all the packages before you start. As soon as a new package has been updated, we will be notified in the Packages folder. To update the package, right-click on the Packages folder and select Update from the contextual menu.

We can create, in the Business subfolder of the Core, the MenuItem class that contains the properties of the available items to order. A MenuItem will have the following:

- Name
- Price
- RequiredSeconds

The class will be developed as follows:

```
public class MenuItem : BaseEntity<int>
{
    public string Name {
        get;
        set;
    }

    public int RequiredSeconds {
        get;
        set;
    }

    public float Price {
        get;
        set;
    }
}
```

We will also prepare the Data Layer element and the Business Layer element for this class using the same structure that we learnt earlier in the book.

In the first instance, they will only use the inheritance with the base classes.

The Data layer will be coded like this:

```
public class MenuItemData : BaseData<MenuItem,int>
{
    public MenuItemData ()
    {
    }
}
```

And the Business layer will look like this:

```
public class MenuItemBusiness : BaseBusiness <MenuItem , int>
{
    public MenuItemBusiness () : base (new MenuItemData ())
    {
    }
}
```

Now we can add a new base class under the `Services` subfolder of the base layer.

Service layer

In this example, we will develop a simple service that makes the request wait for the required time. We will change the base service later in the chapter in order to make server requests.

We will define our Base Service using a generic Base Entity type:

```
public class BaseService<TEntity, TKey>
where TEntity : BaseEntity<TKey>
{
    // we will write here the code for the base service
}
```

Inside the Base Service we need to define an event to throw when the response is ready to be dispatched:

```
public event ResponseReceivedHandler ResponseReceived;

public delegate void ResponseReceivedHandler (TEntity item);
```

We will raise this event when our process has been completed. Before we raise an event we always need to check if it has been subscribed from someone. It is a good practice to use a design pattern called observer.

 A design pattern is a model of solution for common problems and they help us to reuse the design of the software.

To be compliant with the Observer we only need to add to the code we wrote, the following code snippet that raises the event only when the event has been subscribed:

```
protected void OnResponseReceived (TEntity item)
{
    if (ResponseReceived != null) {
        ResponseReceived (item);
    }
}
```

The only thing we need to do in order to raise the `ResponseReceived` event is to call the method `OnResponseReceived`.

Now we will write a base method that gives us a response after a number of seconds that we will pass as a parameter, as seen in the following code:

```
public virtual asyncTask<TEntity>GetDelayedResponse(TEntity item,int
seconds)
{
    await Task.Delay (seconds * 1000);
    OnResponseReceived (item);
    return item;
}
```

We will use this base to simulate a delayed response.

Let's create the Core service layer object for `MenuItem`. We can name it `MenuItemService` and it will inherit the `BaseService`, as follows:

```
public class MenuItemService : BaseService<MenuItem,int>
{
    public MenuItemService ()
    {
    }
}
```

We now have all the core ingredients to start writing our UI.

Add a new empty class named `OrderPage` in the `Presentation` subfolder of Core.

We will insert a label here to read the results, and three buttons to make the requests:

```
public class OrderPage : ContentPage
{
    public OrderPage () : base ()
    {
        Label response = new Label ();
        Button buttonSandwich = new Button
        {
            Text = "Order Sandwich"
        };
        Button buttonSoftdrink = new Button
        {
            Text = "Order Drink"
        };
        Button buttonShowReceipt = new Button
        {
            Text = "Show Receipt"
        };
        // ... insert here the presentation logic
    }
}
```

Presentation Layer

We can now define the presentation logic creating instances of the business object and the service object. We will also define our items:

```
MenuItemBusiness menuManager = new MenuItemBusiness ();
MenuItemService service = new MenuItemService ();

MenuItem sandwich = new MenuItem {
    Name = "Sandwich",
    RequiredSeconds = 10,
    Price = 5
};

MenuItem softdrink = new MenuItem {
    Name = "Sprite",
    RequiredSeconds = 5,
    Price = 2
};
```

Now we need to subscribe the buttons click event to send the order to our service.

The `GetDelayedResponse` method of the service is simulating a slow response. We will develop, later in the chapter, a call to a remote service. In this case, we will have a real delay that depends on the network availability and the time that the remote server needs to process the request and send back a response:

```
buttonSandwich.Clicked += (sender, e) => {
    service.GetDelayedResponse (sandwich, sandwich.RequiredSeconds);

};
buttonSoftdrink.Clicked += (sender,  e) => {

    service.GetDelayedResponse (softdrink, softdrink.RequiredSeconds);
};
```

Our service will raise an event when the response is ready.

We can subscribe this event to present the results on the label and to save the items in our local database:

```
service.ResponseReceived += (item) => {
    // Append the received item to the label
    response.Text +=
    String.Format ("\nReceived: {0} ({1}$)",
    item.Name,
    item.Price);

    // Read the data from the local database
    List<MenuItem> itemlist = menuManager.Read ();

    //calculate the new database key for the item
    item.Key = itemlist.Count == 0 ? 0 : itemlist.Max
    (x => x.Key) + 1;

    //Add The item in the local database
    menuManager.Create (item);
};
```

We now can subscribe the click event of the receipt button in order to display an alert that displays the number of the items saved in the local database and the total price to pay:

```
buttonShowReceipt.Clicked += (object sender, EventArgs e) => {

    List<MenuItem> itemlist = menuManager.Read ();
    float total = itemlist.Sum (x => x.Price);
    DisplayAlert (
        "Receipt",
        String.Format (
            "Total:{0}$ ({1} items)",
            total,
            itemlist.Count),
        "OK");
};
```

The last step is to add the component to the content page:

```
Content = new StackLayout {
    VerticalOptions = LayoutOptions.CenterAndExpand,
    HorizontalOptions = LayoutOptions.CenterAndExpand,
    Children = {
        response,
        buttonSandwich,
        buttonSoftdrink,
        buttonShowReceipt
    }
};
```

At this point we are ready to run the iOS version and to try it out. In order to make the Android version work we need to set the permissions to read and write in the database file.

To do that, we can double-click on the **Droid** project and, in the **Android Application** section, check the **ReadExternalStorage** and **WriteExternalStorage** permissions:

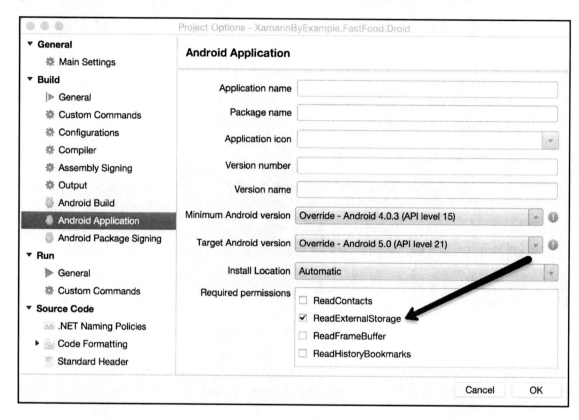

In the `OnCreate` method of the `MainActivity` of the Droid project we also need to:

1. Create the database file when it hasn't been created yet.
2. Set the database path in the Configuration file.

```
var path = System.Environment.GetFolderPath
(System.Environment.SpecialFolder.ApplicationData
);
if (!Directory.Exists (path)) {
  Directory.CreateDirectory (path);
}
var filename = Path.Combine (path, "fastfood.db");
if (!File.Exists (filename)) {
  File.Create (filename);
}
Configuration.DatabasePath = filename;
```

Services

Services are reusable application components shared to other components via a communication protocol, typically over a network. A service can provide more than one operation. The application logic of a service is exposed via **API (Application Program Interface)**. There are two major classes of web service: REST-compliant web services and Arbitrary web services.

When we need our app to write data in a central server or read data from it, we always need to write a service server side that allows us to open a communication channel.

Web Service Description Language

A particular type of Arbitrary web service is described by the **Web Service Description Language (WSDL).** WSDL is an XML-based interface definition language that is used for describing the functionality offered by a web service.

To use a WSDL, we need to right-click on the project and select **Add a Web Reference**:

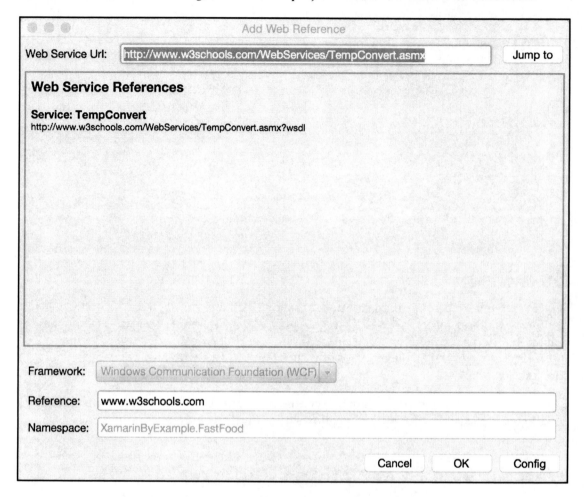

In the web service URL, we have to put the address of the server that provides the web service. Xamarin Studio automatically creates the classes to interface to the service and we can make the available requests to it in our code.

RESTful APIs

REST-compliant web services use a uniform set of stateless operations; typically, it offers CRUD over HTTP.

The communication between a system and a service is based on exchanging messages between the two.

Every time we need to communicate with another system we need to define the following:

- How to request data
- Parameters needed in the request
- Structure of data in the response
- Error messages to display

How to request data
REST APIs use the standard HTTP verbs:

- GET: This is used to retrieve data
- POST: This is used to submit data as a new record
- PUT: This is used to update data in an existing record
- PATCH: This is used to update specific parts of a record
- DELETE: This is used to delete a specific record

In our base service layer, we can add methods to submit all these types of requests.

Parameters needed in the data request
When we send a request to a service, typically we need to retrieve or insert data attaching some parameters to the request.

The server that hosts the APIs will process our parameters and send us back a response.

When we need to call APIs from our mobile solution we need to know the parameters that the server is expecting.

Requests made with the GET method, transfer parameters inside of the URL, such as `http://www.google.com?q=xamarin`.

Requests made with the POST method, transfer parameters inside of `RequestBody`. So, POST method requests hide more parameters from bare eyes than GET method requests.

Developers choose the GET or POST method only, and the transfer of parameters is done by the framework.

Structure of data in response

The communication from RESTful APIs and our app will be based on messages. The messages that we can receive from the APIs contain data that can be delivered in different formats:

- JSON
- XML
- HTML
- Plain text

When we receive a response we need to parse it in order to map the data received into our business logic.

For that reason, we need to study the API documentation provided by the API provider so that we will be able to understand the structure and the meaning of the data received.

Error messages to display

Typically, each REST API gives us a list of possible errors with the description of it. We need to consider that, so that we can manage to give the user the right feedback as a response, even when the transmission of the supposed message fails for some reason.

Example project Weather

We will now create a new Xamarin.Forms (PCL) solution named Weather. It will allow us to write a location in a text box and it will provide the weather condition of the location using an external service provided as RESTful APIs.

We will use the APIs provided from `http://openweathermap.org/api`.

We will start importing all the base code we've written for the previous projects and we can add an empty class called `HTTPHelper` in the `Services` subfolder of the Base layer.

In this class, we will define each method to make a data request:

```
public class HTTPHelper
{
    public HTTPHelper ()
    {
    }

    public async Task<string> GET ( string url )
    {
        return "//To implement";
    }

    public async Task<string> POST ( string url )
    {
        return "//To implement";
    }

    public async Task<string> PUT ( string url )
    {
        return "//To implement";
    }

    public async Task<string> DELETE ( string url )
    {
        return "//To implement";
    }
}
```

We will also add the event to throw when the response has been received:

```
public event ResponseReceivedHandler ResponseReceived;

public delegate void ResponseReceivedHandler (string item);

protected void OnResponseReceived (string item)
{
    if (ResponseReceived != null) {
        ResponseReceived (item);
    }
}
```

Before developing the helper's methods we need to import a new NuGet Package: **Microsoft HTTP Client Libraries**.

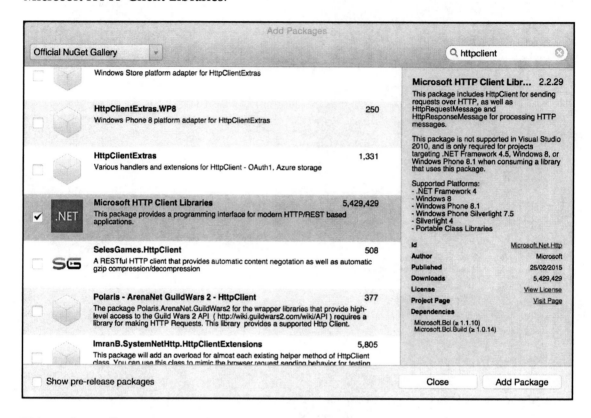

This package allows us to use the `System.Net.Http` namespace, which contains all the classes we need to make async HTTP web requests.

`HttpClient` supports async requests to POST, GET, and DELETE.

When the response has been received we will raise the `ResponseReceived` event:

```
public async Task<string> POST (string url, string data)
{
    using (var client = new HttpClient ()) {
        StringContent content = new StringContent(data);
        var response = await client.PostAsync (url, content);
        string responseBody = await
                        response.Content.ReadAsStringAsync();
        OnResponseReceived (responseBody);
        return responseBody;
    }
}
```

We will develop the GET verb in the same way:

```
public async Task<string> GET (string url)
{
    using (var client = new HttpClient ()) {
        string response = await client.GetStringAsync (url);
        OnResponseReceived (response);
        return response;
    }
}
```

Try to develop the helpers for the verbs PUT and DELETE yourself. You will find the solution in the code attached to the `XamarinByExample.Weather`.

Data model

What we need now is to create a class to define the Weather. To have a guide for it, we can take advantage of the `openweathermap` documentation and wrap some of their JSON responses into C# classes.

To do that, we can find help from some interesting online services such as `http://json2cs harp.com/` that allow us to copy a JSON and generate the C# classes:

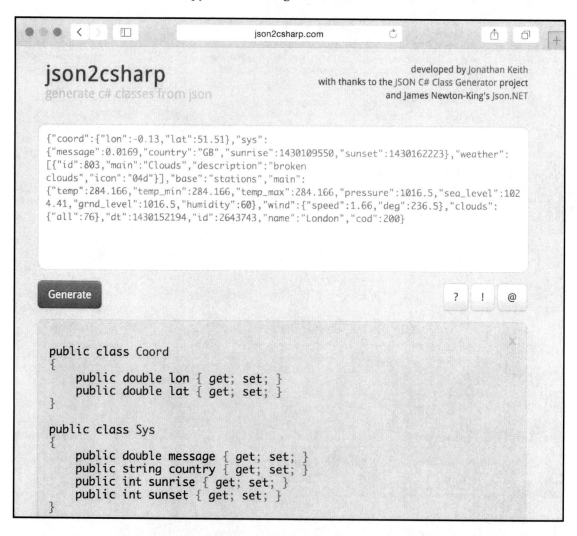

We can make a request to the weather service and paste the response on the data field of `json2csharp`, we will have our C# class touching the **Generate** button.

It will be better to modify the names of the classes and the names of the fields. `Json2csharp` gives us a mapping based on the naming contained in the JSON message.

It is a good practice to keep one class in one file. So we will create one file for each class generated by the tool.

To manage the JSON serialization to our objects we will import a package named `Json.NET` from the NuGet components:

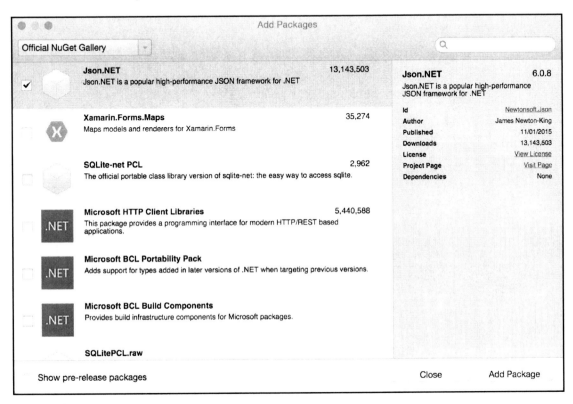

We need to create all the classes and set the `JsonProperty` attribute to them in order to map the JSON response we are expecting from the APIs.

Here's an example of implementation of the `Coordinates` type. We have two properties, which in the JSON file will have the names `lon` and `lat`.

Imagine that we want to call our properties `Latitude` and `Longitude`. What we can do is assign to the `JsonProperty` attribute , a `PropertyName` that maps the field we expect to receive:

```
public class Coordinates
{
    [JsonProperty(PropertyName = "lon")]
```

```
        public double Longitude { get; set; }

        [JsonProperty(PropertyName = "lat")]
        public double Latitude { get; set; }
    }
```

When we finish mapping all the classes, we can create the root object and name it
`WeatherConditions`:

```
    public class WeatherConditions : BaseEntity<int>
    {
        [JsonProperty(PropertyName = "coord")]
        public Coordinates Coordinates { get; set; }

        [JsonProperty(PropertyName = "sys")]
        public Sys Sys { get; set; }

        [JsonProperty(PropertyName = "weather")]
        public List<Weather> Weather { get; set; }

        [JsonProperty(PropertyName = "base")]
        public string Base { get; set; }

        [JsonProperty(PropertyName = "main")]
        public Main Main { get; set; }

        [JsonProperty(PropertyName = "wind")]
        public Wind Wind { get; set; }

        [JsonProperty(PropertyName = "clouds")]
        public Clouds Clouds { get; set; }

        [JsonProperty(PropertyName = "dt")]
        public int Dt { get; set; }

        [JsonProperty(PropertyName = "id")]
        public int Id { get; set; }

        [JsonProperty(PropertyName = "name")]
        public string Name { get; set; }

        [JsonProperty(PropertyName = "cod")]
        public int Cod { get; set; }
    }
```

`WeatherConditions` **will inherit BaseEntity so it can take advantage of all our base classes.**

Service layer

We will now focus on modifying the `BaseService` class.

It would be great to have a generic `BaseService` that uses `HttpHelper` to retrieve the data and parse our JSON into our model.

First, we will add a private read-only property that will contain the object of our `httpHelper` to our `BaseService` class:

```
readonly HttpHelper httpHelper;
```

We will instance it on our constructor:

```
public BaseService ()
{
    httpHelper = new HttpHelper ();
}
```

Now we will replace the method we've created as an example with the calls to the helper. We will make the call with the helper and then we will deserialize the received JSON in our entity by using the `Json.NET` library facilities. To use them, we need to use the `Newtonsoft.Json` namespace:

```
public async Task<TEntity> GET (string url)
{
    string response = await httpHelper.GET (url);
    TEntity item = JsonConvert.DeserializeObject<TEntity> (response);
    OnResponseReceived (item);
    return item;
}
```

Similarly, we will also develop the `POST`, `PUT`, and `DELETE` methods.

Now we can add, in the `Services` subfolder of `Core`, a new empty object named `WeatherContitionsService`.

This object will inherit from the `BaseService` class:

```
public class WeatherConditionsService :
BaseService<WeatherConditions,int>
```

As an example, we can create a method to search the weather conditions of a query passed as a parameter. As we can see, to develop this method we can now use all the facilities we've developed on our `BaseService`:

```
public async Task<WeatherConditions> SearchWeather (string query)
{
    string url = "http://api.openweathermap.org/data/2.5/weather?q=" +
query;
    WeatherConditions item = await GET (url);
    return item;
}
```

Once our service is developed, we can now write a simple UI with a textbox and a button to download the weather conditions of the place written on the textbox from our user.

Presentation layer

We can create, in the `Presentation` folder, a new Content Page named `WeatherSearchPage`.

We will add the input box and the button:

```
Entry inputText = new Entry ();
Button searchButton = new Button {
    Text = "Search"
};
```

And we can assign them as children of a StackLayout to assign to the `Content` property of the page:

```
Content = new StackLayout {
    Children = { inputText, searchButton }
};
```

We will create an instance of the Weather Service and we will subscribe the `ResponseReceived` event to display some results. In the example, we want to manage it showing an alert with the temperature received from the service:

```
WeatherConditionsService service =
  new WeatherConditionsService ();
service.ResponseReceived += (item) => {
    DisplayAlert (
        "Temperature",
        item.Main.Temperature.ToString (),
        "OK");
};
```

As the last step, we can subscribe to the `Clicked` event of the `searchButton` in order to call the `SearchWeather` method of our service object, giving as input the query written from the user in the textbox:

```
searchButton.Clicked += (sender, e) => {
    service.SearchWeather (inputText.Text);
};
```

Ideas

In the Xamarin world, we have AppLinks to talk to other applications that are also installed on the device.

AppLink handles differences between iOS, Android, and other platforms. We can add incoming and outgoing AppLink support to our projects.

In order to add support for launching our project by another application, we need to add a protocol for our application. In Xamarin.Forms iOS projects we can define the URL scheme; in Xamarin.Forms Android projects we can define the DataScheme. In that way, other applications make a request to, let's say, `example://showlist?category=all` URL, and launch our application with showlist and `category=all` parameters.

In order to launch another app with some parameters, we have to know the application's AppLink scheme URL and parameters. If we make a request to, let's say, `maps://europe?country=turkey`, the default maps application will launch with Turkey in view.

Summary

In this chapter, we discussed communication. We learned how to work in an asynchronous context, developing an example of a cross-platform app that simulates a fast food restaurant.

We used an async context in a base service to make HTTP requests to REST APIs and we also used open weather APIs to make a cross-platform app that shows us the weather conditions in a place that the user can select. In the next chapter, we'll write custom renderers to customize screen components.

6
Custom Renderers

Xamarin is a framework that allows us to write most of the UI code in a platform-agnostic style. In this chapter, we will understand how `Xamarin.Forms` does it and how we can create our own platform agnostic components, providing them a platform-specific appearance.

Rendering model

So far, our point of view has been focused on developing solutions using the `Xamarin.Forms.Core` libraries, creating our own shareable or PCL projects. The `Xamarin.Forms.Core` library uses the platform-specific `Xamarin.Forms.Platform` libraries. These libraries are a collection of classes called renderers. Each renderer transforms the agnostic elements in a platform specific user interface.

For example, suppose we need a user interface object that allows the user to manipulate a horizontal bar in order to choose a numeric value.

`Xamarin.Forms.Core` contains an element named Slider that does this. In the renderers contained in the `Xamarin.Forms.Platform` libraries, the Slider is mapped as UISlider on the iPhone, SeekBar on Android, and Slider on Windows Phone.

These components will have a different appearance on the three platforms because they are all rendered with the object specific to each platform.

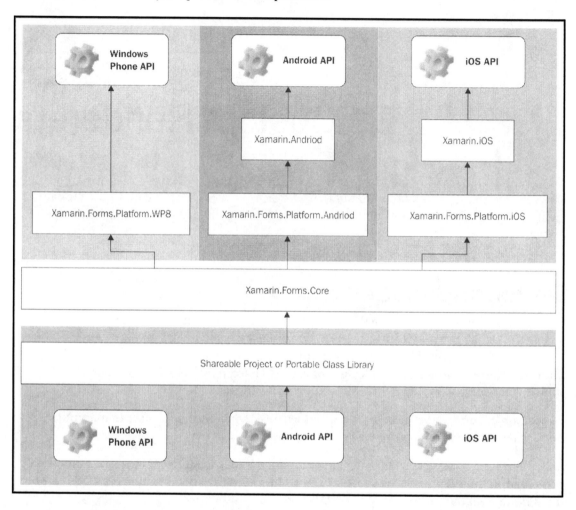

As we can see in the preceding diagram, platform-specific apps use each platform's native API layers.

The `Xamarin.Forms.Core` layer adds abstraction to UI elements. With this abstraction, we can develop a page using Xaml. `Xamarin.Forms` translates Xaml and uses the platform's native elements.

The shareable project or PCL layer is optional and adds reusable classes to our projects.

On top of everything below, we can develop our UI layer.

When our application executes in a platform, the platform-specific renderer takes control of elements, turning them into something visual for the platform.

Each renderer is platform-specific and is not shareable.

Custom renderers

We can create our own custom visual objects with our own custom renderers. The custom visual object will be available in the common code project and will have a custom renderer in each individual platform project.

We can also derive from existing renderers. All the renderers of the Xamarin.Forms framework are public and we are allowed to inherit them on our own renderers.

> Xamarin.Forms is not a complete replacement for native APIs. There are features unique to particular platforms that are not implemented in Xamarin.Forms.
> When choosing whether or not to use Xamarin.Forms, we need to consider that. In the case that our app is based on native API features, it will be better to use Xamarin.iOS, Xamarin.Android, and the native Windows Phone API.
> The use of Xamarin.Forms is also not suggested (at the moment) if we require vector graphics or complex touch interactions.

Now we will implement a component that takes an image and turns it into a circle with a border.

Rounded image example

Currently there's no common element in the framework that allows us to transform an image into a circle. To create it, we need to deal with Custom Renderers.

We will create a new element named Rounded Image, which we can use in our common code.

First of all, we need to create a new `Xamarin.Forms` project. Let's name it `CustomRenderers`.

The common project will be named `CustomRenderers` and the Xamarin templates manager will create `CustomRenderers.iOS` and `CustomRenderers.Android` for us.

We now need to create a class named `RoundedImage` in the common core.

We can derive it from the base class `Image`:

```
using Xamarin.Forms;

namespace CustomRenderers
{
    public class RoundedImage : Image
    {
        public RoundedImage ()
        {
        }
    }
}
```

In order to build custom renderers for it, we need to add our renderers to the platform specific projects.

Let's create an empty class for each platform named `RoundedImageRenderer`.

We can derive the `RoundedImageRenderer` from the `ImageRenderer` after all, we need to transform the image in a platform-specific view and `ImageRenderer` already does it for us.

The implementation of it will start with something like this for iOS:

```
using Xamarin.Forms.Platform.iOS;

namespace CustomRenderers.iOS
{
    public class RoundedImageRenderer : ImageRenderer
    {
        public RoundedImageRenderer ()
        {
        }
    }
}
```

For Android, it will start like this:

```
using Xamarin.Forms.Platform.Android;

namespace CustomRenderers.Droid
{
    public class RoundedImageRenderer : ImageRenderer
    {
        public RoundedImageRenderer ()
        {
        }
    }
}
```

We now need to write the platform-specific method to make a circle around the image.

We can add a private method named `CreateCircle` that can do it with platform specific code.

This method can use the `Control` property of the base `ImageRenderer`, that is, in this context a platform-specific control: `UIImageView`.

In iOS, we can set the border to be a rounded border with a corner radius of half of the minor dimension of the image. This way we will have a bordered circle around our image:

```
private void CreateCircle ()
{
    double min = Math.Min (Element.Width, Element.Height);
    Control.Layer.CornerRadius = (float)(min / 2.0);
    Control.Layer.MasksToBounds = false;
    Control.Layer.BorderColor = UIKit.UIColor.Blue.CGColor;
    Control.Layer.BorderWidth = 4;
    Control.ClipsToBounds = true;
}
```

Later in this chapter, we'll need to override the `OnElementChanged` method and call the `CreateCircle` method inside it.

The last thing to do is to define the `ExportRenderer` attribute that will bind our platform-agnostic object to the platform-specific object:

```
[assembly: ExportRenderer (typeof(RoundedImage),
typeof(RoundedImageRenderer))]
```

We can now develop the Android renderer.

On the Android platform, we need to override the `DrawChild` method to manually draw a circle to clip the image, and a circle as the border to draw:

```
protected override bool DrawChild (Canvas canvas, Android.Views.View child,
long drawingTime)
{
    var radius = Math.Min (Width, Height) / 2;

    var strokeWidth = 10;
    radius -= strokeWidth / 2;

    Path path = new Path ();
    path.AddCircle (Width / 2,
                    Height / 2,
                    radius,
                    Path.Direction.Ccw);
    canvas.Save ();
    canvas.ClipPath (path);

    var result = base.DrawChild(canvas, child, drawingTime);

    canvas.Restore ();

    path = new Path ();
    path.AddCircle (Width / 2,
                    Height / 2,
                    radius,
                    Path.Direction.Ccw);

    var paint = new Paint ();
    paint.AntiAlias = true;
    paint.StrokeWidth = 10;
    paint.SetStyle (Paint.Style.Stroke);
    paint.Color = Android.Graphics.Color.Yellow;

    canvas.DrawPath (path, paint);

    paint.Dispose ();
    path.Dispose ();

    return result;
}
```

In this case, we also need to export the renderers added before the namespace in the attribute:

```
[assembly: ExportRenderer (typeof(RoundedImage),
typeof(RoundedImageRenderer))]
```

We may want to also override the OnElementChanged method. The OnElementChanged method is called when the corresponding Xamarin.Forms control is created. If we call the Invalidate method inside the OnElementChanged method, the Android platform forces to call the DrawChild method. So, we can force to call the DrawChild method when the Xamarin.Forms control is created:

```
protected override void OnElementChanged (ElementChangedEventArgs<Image> e)
{
    base.OnElementChanged (e);
    this.Invalidate ();
}
```

We are now ready to use our RoundedImage control from the common core project, CustomRenderers.

To test our component, we can modify the existing CustomRender.cs, adding the RoundedImage as the only Children in the StackLayout that has been assigned to the Content of the page from the Xamarin template manager:

```
MainPage = new ContentPage {
    Content = new StackLayout {
        Orientation = StackOrientation.Horizontal,
        VerticalOptions = LayoutOptions.Center,
        HorizontalOptions = LayoutOptions.Center,
        Children = {
            new RoundedImage (){
                Source = "avatar.png",
                WidthRequest = 100,
                HeightRequest = 100 }
        }
    }
};
```

When running the app on both platforms, we can see the result of our custom renderers:

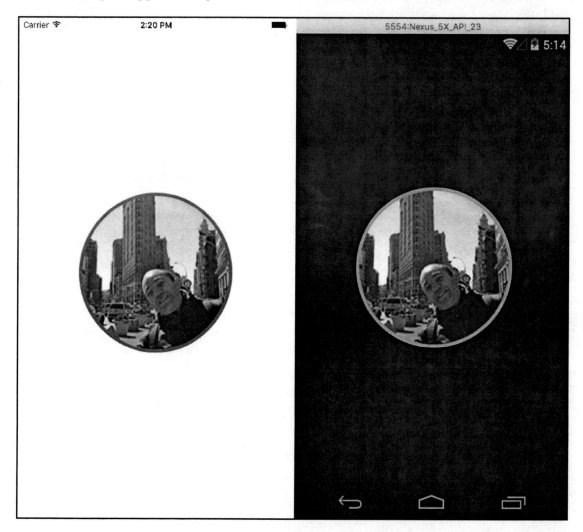

App linking example

Sometimes we might need to write a renderer in order to use features that are not available in the Xamarin.Forms framework. One example of that is App Links.

App Links is a way to link our app with other apps or to handle our app's incoming links. Let's develop a solution that allows us to insert a phone number inside our app and make a call with the Skype app when installed in the user device.

In our CustomRenderers core project, we can create a new Content page that contains an entry box to insert the phone number and a button that will redirect us to the Skype app.

We will also create an event that will transform the click on the button as a `Call` event, passing the phone number to call:

```
public class SkypeCallPage : ContentPage
{
    public event CallHandler Call;

    public delegate void CallHandler (string number);

    public void OnCall (string number)
    {
        if (Call != null) {
            Call (number);
        }
    }

    public SkypeCallPage ()
    {
        Entry phoneNumber = new Entry () {
            HorizontalOptions = LayoutOptions.FillAndExpand,
            Placeholder = "insert a phone number"
        };
        Button call = new Button () {
            HorizontalOptions = LayoutOptions.FillAndExpand,
            Text = "Call"
        };
        call.Clicked += (object sender, EventArgs e) =>
            OnCall (phoneNumber.Text);

        Content = new StackLayout {
            Orientation = StackOrientation.Vertical,
            VerticalOptions = LayoutOptions.Center,
            HorizontalOptions = LayoutOptions.Center,
            Children = {
                phoneNumber, call
            }
        };
    }
}
```

We now need to implement the renderer of the `SkypeCallPage` in the platform-specific projects. We will follow the Skype documentation in order to make the link between our app and the Skype app.

We will start with the iOS version of the renderer. The documentation on how to integrate an iOS app with Skype can be found at `https://msdn.microsoft.com/EN-US/library/office/dn745885.aspx`.

We need to subscribe the Call event from the `SkypeCallPage` that we will find in the `Element` property of the `PageRenderer`.

In the override of the `OnElementChanged` method, we have to include the call to the Skype app passing in the URL the number that we want to call:

```
public class SkypeCallPageRenderer : PageRenderer
{
    protected override void OnElementChanged (VisualElementChangedEventArgs e)
    {
        base.OnElementChanged (e);
        SkypeCallPage page = (Element as SkypeCallPage);
        page.Call += Page_Call;
    }

    void Page_Call (string number)
    {
        Foundation.NSUrl url = new Foundation.NSUrl ("skype:"
        + number);
        bool installed = UIApplication.SharedApplication
        .CanOpenUrl (url);
        if (installed) {
            UIApplication.SharedApplication.OpenUrl (url);
        } else {
            UIApplication.SharedApplication.OpenUrl (
                new Foundation.NSUrl
                ("http://itunes.com/apps/skype/skype"));
        }
    }
}
```

We always need to add the attribute, `ExportRenderer`, in order to bind the platform-specific behavior with the core library:

```
[assembly: ExportRenderer (typeof(SkypeCallPage),
typeof(SkypeCallPageRenderer))]
```

In Android, we need to follow the documentation available at `https://msdn.microsoft.com/EN-US/library/office/dn745884.aspx`.

The component package name we need to use is `com.skype.raider` and the main activity we need to run is called `com.skype.raider.Main`:

```
public class SkypeCallPageRenderer : PageRenderer
{
    string packageName = "com.skype.raider";
    string componentMainActivity = "com.skype.raider.Main";
    ...
}
```

As per iOS, we need to override the `OnElementChanged` method of `PageRenderer` and subscribe the event:

```
protected override void OnElementChanged (ElementChangedEventArgs<Page> e)
{
    base.OnElementChanged (e);
    SkypeCallPage skypeCallPage = (Element as SkypeCallPage);
    skypeCallPage.Call += SkypeCallPage_Call;
}
```

We can handle the event first by checking if the Skype app is installed in the mobile phone of the user, and moving them to the market in the case that the app has not been installed.

We then need to build the Skype URL composed by the string `skype:`, followed by the number we want to call.

After having done that, we just need to build the intent with the Skype URI and set the component with the Skype app package name and component class name:

```
void SkypeCallPage_Call (string number)
{
    // Make sure the Skype for Android client is installed.
    if (!IsSkypeClientInstalled (Context)) {
        GoToMarket (Context);
        return;
    }
    string mySkypeUri = "skype:" + number;

    // Create the Intent from our Skype URI.
    Uri skypeUri = Uri.Parse (mySkypeUri);
    Intent myIntent = new Intent (Intent.ActionView, skypeUri);

    // Restrict the Intent to being handled by the Skype
    for Android client only.
```

```
myIntent.SetComponent (new ComponentName (packageName,
componentMainActivity));
myIntent.SetFlags (ActivityFlags.NewTask);

// Initiate the Intent. It should never fail because
you've already established the
// presence of its handler (although there is an extremely
minute window where that
// handler can go away).
Context.StartActivity (myIntent);

}
```

In order to determine if the Skype client is installed, we can use the
`PackageManager.GetPackageInfo` **method:**

```
public bool IsSkypeClientInstalled (Context myContext)
{
    PackageManager myPackageMgr = myContext.PackageManager;
    try {
        myPackageMgr.GetPackageInfo (packageName,
        PackageInfoFlags.Activities);
    } catch (PackageManager.NameNotFoundException) {
        return (false);
    }
    return (true);
}
```

If the Skype client is not installed; our app will direct our user to the Android Market
(Google Play Store). To do that, our app can use a `market:` scheme Intent to navigate
directly to the Skype for Android install page:

```
public void GoToMarket (Context myContext)
{
    Uri marketUri =
      Uri.Parse ("market://details?id=com.skype.raider");

    Intent myIntent =
              new Intent (Intent.ActionView, marketUri);

    myIntent.SetFlags (ActivityFlags.NewTask);
    myContext.StartActivity (myIntent);
    return;
}
```

Summary

In this chapter, we've learnt how `Xamarin.Forms` manages the platform-specific elements from the core platform agnostic library. We've built our own renderer to provide a circular image to Android and iOS. We've also explored how to link a third-party app to our solution.

With CustomRenderers we can easily develop components shown specifically in each platform.

In the next chapter, we'll learn about image processing in the `Xamarin.Forms` world with an example project. We'll start with creating the project and developing the entire application.

7
Monkey Puzzle Game – Processing Images

We can imagine images as rectangular arrays (bitmaps) of elements (pixels).

In Xamarin.Forms, bitmaps can be displayed by a view named Image. Different platforms have different ways to manage bitmaps.

Each platform has its own design guideline and the required formats and sizes can be different.

In this chapter, we will develop a simple game step by step that's based on image processing. Talking about images, we will also cover the design guidelines platform by platform for the icons and images.

Monkey Puzzle Game

We will develop a classic 14-15 puzzle using a monkey image.

The game will contain a Start button, a chronometer, and a tiled image.

After pressing the Start button, the user will just tap a tile to move it into an empty position.

The user will use the numbers in the lower-right corner of each tile as a guide.

When the user successfully completes the puzzle, they will be rewarded with a popup.

We will start developing a prototype and then we will add features to this prototype in order to explore the Xamarin.Forms capabilities with images.

In the next chapter, we will also use this project to explore Bluetooth communication.

Starting up – the first prototype

We need to create a new Xamarin.Forms PCL solution named MonkeyPuzzle:

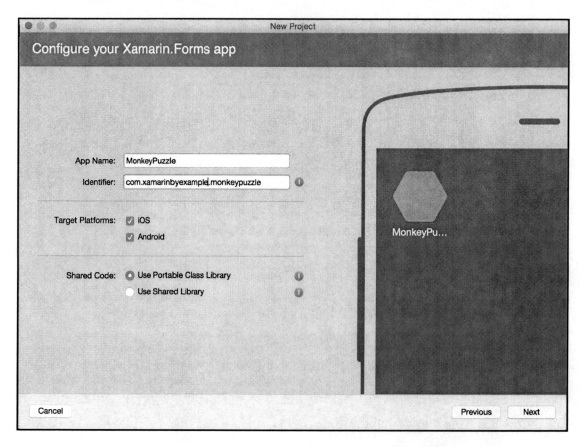

As we've learnt before, Xamarin Studio Template will prepare four projects:

- `MonkeyPuzzle` is the Xamarin.Forms project
- `MonkeyPuzzle.Droid` is the Android-specific project
- `MonkeyPuzzle.iOS` is the iOS-specific project
- `MonkeyPuzzle.UITests` is the test project

We will now focus on developing the core of our game in the `MonkeyPuzzle` project.

The first class we are going to create is the single box that will contain a portion of the image.

We will call it `PuzzleBox`. It will inherit from the `ContentView` base class and it will contain the index and the images needed for all the status of the box as properties:

```
public class PuzzleBox : ContentView
    {
        public int Index {
            get;
            set;
        }


        public Image NormalImage {
            get;
            set;
        }

        public PuzzleBox ()
        {
        }
    }
}
```

We will define a constructor that takes the index and the images as input parameters:

```
public PuzzleBox (Image normal, Image winner, int index)
{
    Index = index;
    NormalImage = normal;
    winner = winner;

    ShownImage = new Image {
        Source = NormalImage.Source
    };

    this.Content = new Frame {
        OutlineColor = Color.Accent,
        Content = new StackLayout {
            Children = {
                ShownImage
            }
        }
    };

    this.BackgroundColor = Color.Transparent;
}
```

Next step will be to develop the page that will contain the puzzle, the button to start a new game, and the stopwatch.

The approach we will follow in the first instance is to separate the image into 16 sub-images, saving each one of them as local resources for the Xamarin.Forms main project.

When our images are saved on the PCL project, we can assign the property using the static method `FromResource` of the class `ImageSource`.

Before that, we need to import our images in the PCL project.

We can now add a `Resources` folder to the common PCL project and drag an image to this folder.

We now need to click on the image and change the build action of the file to `EmbeddedResource` from the **Properties** pad:

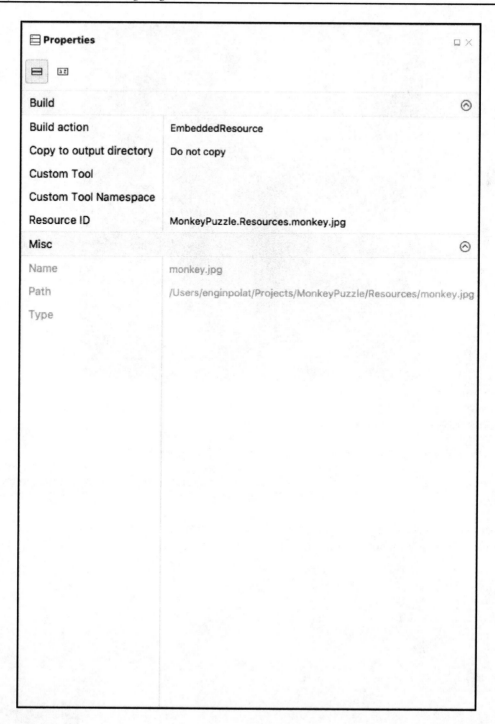

We now need to copy the Resource ID because we need to pass it as a parameter in the `FromResource` method. When we start the app, we will see the common image in each separate platform.

As we can see, this approach allows us to use a platform independent bitmap.

Another way we can show a platform independent bitmap is by using the `FromUri` static method of the class `ImageSource`.

This method allows us to access a bitmap saved somewhere in the Web:

```
Source = ImageSource.FromUri("https://goo.gl/OdXkWQ")
```

The `FromUri` method of the `ImageSource` class spends some extra time to save results to the local cache folder. By caching results to the local folder, it saves precious time to load it from the cache instead of getting it from a server later. If we do not want to use the cache, simply turn it off by setting `CachingEnabled = to false` inside the `UriImageSource` class.

When the URL is not found, the image doesn't appear and this will not raise any exceptions.

We can now create the page and we will call it `PuzzlePage`:

```
public class PuzzlePage : ContentPage
{
    // Number of squares horizontally and vertically,
    //  but if you change it, some code will break.
    static readonly int NUM = 4;

    // Array of PuzzleBox views, and empty row & column.
    PuzzleBox[,] squares = new PuzzleBox[NUM, NUM];
    int emptyRow = NUM - 1;
    int emptyCol = NUM - 1;

    public PuzzlePage (){

    }
}
```

In the constructor, we first need to define an absolute layout where to position all the Puzzle Boxes:

```
// AbsoluteLayout to host the squares.
absoluteLayout = new AbsoluteLayout () {
    HorizontalOptions = LayoutOptions.Center,
    VerticalOptions = LayoutOptions.Center
};
```

Then, we will define an array of images to save each one of the pieces of the puzzle:

```
// Create PuzzleBox's for all the rows and columns.
Image[] normalImages = new Image[NUM * NUM];
```

In a cycle, we will create an instance of each single image and instantiate the puzzle box, saving its row and the column:

```
int index = 0;

for (int row = 0; row < NUM; row++) {
    for (int col = 0; col < NUM; col++) {
        // But skip the last one!
        if (row == NUM - 1 && col == NUM - 1)
            break;
        // Instantiate the image reading it from the local resources.
        normalImages [index] = new Image ();
        normalImages [index].Source = ImageSource
        .FromResource( String.Format("MonkeyPuzzle.{0}.png", index + 1));

        // Instantiate PuzzleBox.
        PuzzleBox square = new PuzzleBox (normalImages [index], index) {
            Row = row,
            Col = col
        };

        // Add here tap recognition

        // Add it to the array and the AbsoluteLayout.
        squares [row, col] = square;
        absoluteLayout.Children.Add (square);
        index++;
    }
}
```

We now need to add a tap recognizer in order to manage the touch on a single box element:

```
TapGestureRecognizer tapGestureRecognizer =
        new TapGestureRecognizer {
            Command = new Command (OnSquareTapped),
            CommandParameter = square
        };
        square.GestureRecognizers.Add (tapGestureRecognizer);
```

In the `OnSquareTapped` method, we will write the logic to shift the square into an empty position.

First, we need to code the animation of the square.

We need to move a PuzzleBox from the current row and column to a new one.

To animate it, we will use the `LayoutTo` method, which is one of the extension methods for Views in `Xamarin.Forms`.

 The `LayoutTo` method comes with `Xamarin.Forms` and it's actually an extension method of `VisualElement`. We may use the `LayoutTo` method with any `VisualElement`, as we want to animate transitions between layout states that changes its size or position. It's usable if we need to animate visual elements, size, or position changes easily. Alternatively, we may use `FadeTo`, `RotateTo`, `ScaleTo`, and other methods as well.

`ViewExtensions` provide views with animated scaling, rotation, and layout functions:

```
async Task AnimateSquare (int row,
                          int col,
                          int newRow,
                          int newCol
                          )
{
    // The Square to be animated.
    PuzzleBox animaSquare = squares [row, col];

    // The destination rectangle.
    Rectangle rect = new Rectangle (squareSize * emptyCol,
        squareSize * emptyRow,
        squareSize,
        squareSize);

    // This is the actual animation call.
    await animaSquare.LayoutTo (rect, 100);
}
```

We can now write the logic to shift the squares into the empty position.

When it happens, if in the same row or column of the tapped element there is the empty box, the tapped element will be empty and all the elements in the row or column will shift away:

```
async Task ShiftIntoEmpty (int tappedRow, int tappedCol)
{
    // Shift columns.
    if (tappedRow == emptyRow && tappedCol != emptyCol) {
        int inc = Math.Sign (tappedCol - emptyCol);
        int begCol = emptyCol + inc;
        int endCol = tappedCol + inc;

        for (int col = begCol; col != endCol; col += inc) {
            await AnimateSquare (emptyRow, col, emptyRow, emptyCol);
        }
    }
    // Shift rows.
    else if (tappedCol == emptyCol && tappedRow != emptyRow) {
        int inc = Math.Sign (tappedRow - emptyRow);
        int begRow = emptyRow + inc;
        int endRow = tappedRow + inc;

        for (int row = begRow; row != endRow; row += inc) {
            await AnimateSquare (row, emptyCol, emptyRow, emptyCol);
        }
    }
}
```

Now we have everything we need to write our `OnSquareTapped` method.

We will check here whether the move makes the player a winner, or if it needs to just shift the boxes into the empty position:

```
async void OnSquareTapped (object parameter)
{
    PuzzleBox tappedSquare = (PuzzleBox)parameter;
    await ShiftIntoEmpty (tappedSquare.Row, tappedSquare.Col);

    // Check for a "win".
        int index;

        for (index = 0; index < NUM * NUM - 1; index++) {
            int row = index / NUM;
            int col = index % NUM;
            PuzzleBox square = squares [row, col];
            if (square == null || square.Index != index)
```

```
                break;
        }

    // We have a winner!
    if (index == NUM * NUM - 1) {
      isPlaying = false;
      await DisplayAlert ("CONGRATULATION", "YOU WON","OK");
      }
    }
  }
```

As we can see in the preceding code, we implemented the OnSquareTapped method to detect whether the user has solved the puzzle or not. We basically loop through all the cells and check its index if it is correct or wrong. If all the cells are in the correct index, then we display the winning message.

We almost have all the pieces we need to run the game.

The last few things that we need in order to build our first prototype are the stopwatch and a button to start the game and randomize the elements.

For the stopwatch, we can use the static method named StartTimer of the Device class.

It will start a recurring timer using the device clock capabilities:

```
Device.StartTimer (TimeSpan.FromSeconds (1), () => {
    // Round duration and get rid of milliseconds.
    TimeSpan timeSpan = (DateTime.Now - startTime) +
        TimeSpan.FromSeconds (0.5);
    timeSpan = new TimeSpan (timeSpan.Hours, timeSpan.Minutes,
    timeSpan.Seconds);

    // Display the duration.
    if (isPlaying)
        timeLabel.Text = timeSpan.ToString ("t");
    return isPlaying;
});
```

To stop the timer, we will switch the flag to isPlaying.

To randomize the puzzle, we can simulate a sequence of fast crazy taps in a cycle:

```
for (int i = 0; i < 100; i++) {
    await ShiftIntoEmpty (rand.Next (NUM), emptyCol, 25);
    await ShiftIntoEmpty (emptyRow, rand.Next (NUM), 25);
}
```

The following screenshot shows us the start of the puzzle game, the image is mixed, the timer is started, and we can make moves:

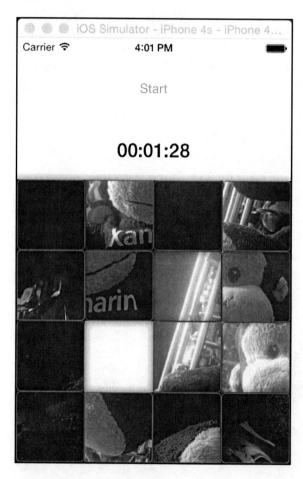

As we can see in the following screenshot, the puzzle game detects that a player won the game. All squares (cells) are in the correct position:

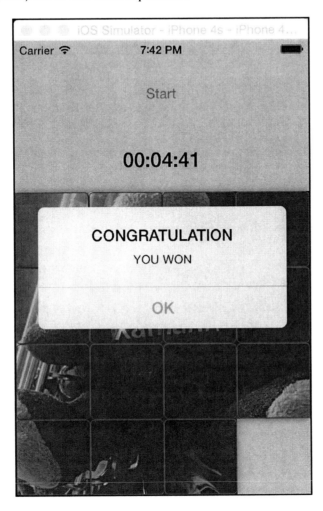

We now have the prototype of our puzzle game.

We will write some enhancement in order to make it better and learn how to work with images.

Loading images from the Web

We will now load an image from a url and process it in order to use it in the game.

As we saw before, to load an image from the web is not difficult, and we can use this statement:

```
Source = ImageSource.FromUri("https://goo.gl/OdXkWQ")
```

What we need to learn is how to process that image in order to make it square, and to split it in the matrix that each single element of the puzzle needs.

Unfortunately, `Xamarin.Forms` does not provide a cross-platform crop method.

For this reason, we need to define our own cross-platform custom image and specify the behavior in each platform-specific project defining the renderers.

We will first add a new definition of the image named `PuzzleImage` in the `MonkeyPuzzle` project.

We will add a field named `MatrixField` to the Image defined in the `Xamarin.Forms` framework:

```
using Xamarin.Forms;

namespace MonkeyPuzzle
{
    public class PuzzleImage : Image
    {
        public Image[,] MatrixImage { get; set;}

        public PuzzleImage ()
        {
        }
    }
}
```

Let's now add the renderers to the platform-specific project. We will name them `PuzzleImageRenderer`, and they both will inherit from `ImageRenderer`.

It's very important to define the decoration to export the renderer before any namespace declaration:

```
[assembly: ExportRenderer(typeof(PuzzleImage),typeof(PuzzleImageRenderer))]
```

In Android, we need to override the void method, `OnElementChanged`.

Inside this method, we need to first parse the element as `PuzzleImage` to have access to the `MatrixImage` field:

```
PuzzleImage originalImage = e.OldElement as PuzzleImage;
```

Now we can prepare the handler, assuming that it will arrive from a URL resource:

```
IImageSourceHandler handler;

if (originalImage.Source is UriImageSource) {
    handler = new ImageLoaderSourceHandler ();
} else {
    throw new NotImplementedException ();
}
```

Then we can load the image from the given source:

```
 var originalBitmap = await handler.LoadImageAsync (originalImage.Source,
Context);
```

We have to transform the image into a square, looking for the smaller dimension and creating a final bitmap sized with the minimum dimension:

```
using (Bitmap bitmap = originalBitmap) {
    //transforms the image in a square
    int minDimension = 0;
    if (bitmap.Height <= bitmap.Width) {
        minDimension = bitmap.Height;
    } else {
        minDimension = bitmap.Width;
    }

    Bitmap finalBitmap = null;
    finalBitmap = Bitmap.CreateBitmap (bitmap, 0, 0, minDimension,
    minDimension);
    ...//to continue
}
```

The using clause manages to dispose the bitmap.

The using() code block is a compiler trick, actually. When the compiler sees the using() block, it removes it from the code and simply adds the Dispose() method to the variable instantiated inside of the using() block. It is a safe coding trick and frees the developer to call the Dispose() method implicitly, compiler securely calls it. It makes it easy to prevent memory leaks due to not calling the Dispose() method.

We now need to populate the matrix with the portions of the image we need to set as images in the PuzzleBoxes.

We will calculate the size of the image in a single square and then we will iterate the image cropping until we reach the dimension of the puzzle (4 x 4):

```
int squareSize = minDimension / 4;
originalImage.MatrixImage = new Image[4, 4];
for (int col = 0; col < 4; col++) {
    for (int row = 0; row < 4; row++) {
        Bitmap bmp = Bitmap.CreateBitmap (finalBitmap, row * squareSize,
col * squareSize, minDimension, minDimension);
        originalImage.MatrixImage [row, col] = new Image () {
            Source = ImageSource.FromStream (() => {
                MemoryStream ms = new MemoryStream ();
                bmp.Compress (Bitmap.CompressFormat.Jpeg, 100, ms);
                ms.Seek (0L, SeekOrigin.Begin);
                return ms;
            })
        };
    }
}
```

We will follow almost the same process for iOS and Windows, with the difference that we will use the platform-specific framework in order to split the image.

Let's add the iOS renderer:

```
[assembly: ExportRenderer (typeof(PuzzleImage),
typeof(PuzzleImageRenderer))]
namespace MonkeyPuzzle.iOS
{
    public class PuzzleImageRenderer : ImageRenderer
    {
        public PuzzleImageRenderer ()
        {
        }
    }
}
```

We need to override the OnElementChanged method of the renderer.

In this method, we will write the code to crop the image and save it in the Matrix property.

Taking pictures and loading an image from the gallery

In theory, in order to load an image from the gallery, we need to write another renderer and write the platform-specific code that does it in each platform.

Fortunately, there is an open source framework named XLabs, which provides a powerful and cross-platform set of controls and helpers tailored to work with Xamarin.Forms.

XLabs contains a service named Camera that includes taking a picture and selecting a picture from the gallery.

We need to add the `Xamarin.Form.Labs` reference to our projects from the NuGet package manager:

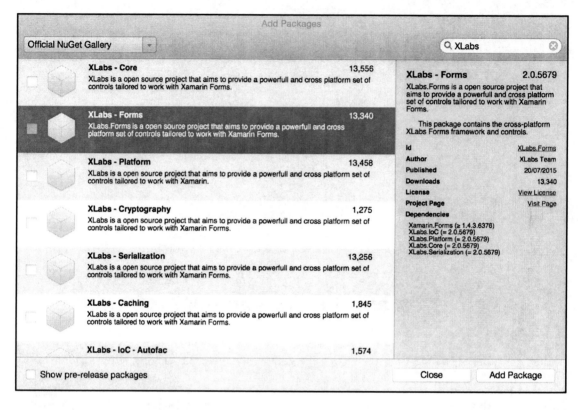

We can include this functionality as a method in our custom `PuzzleImage` image.

Inside the method, we first need to define and get a `MediaPicker` and then use the `SelectPhoto` method in order to get the `ImageSource` of the selected image:

```
public async Task LoadFromGallery(){
    var mediaPicker = DependencyService.Get<IMediaPicker> ();
    ImageSource = null;
    try {
        var mediaFile = await mediaPicker.SelectPhotoAsync
        (new CameraMediaStorageOptions {
            DefaultCamera = CameraDevice.Front,
            MaxPixelDimension = 400
        });
        this.Source = ImageSource.FromStream(() => mediaFile.Source);
        } catch (System.Exception ex) {
        }
}
```

This code will already work cross platform because the Dependency Services are written in the XLabs project that we've referenced.

We can go ahead and use the camera on the device to take the picture to include in the game.

In this case, we need to set the Androidpermission for the camera and the storage. We can do that by double-clicking on the Android project and setting it from the settings window:

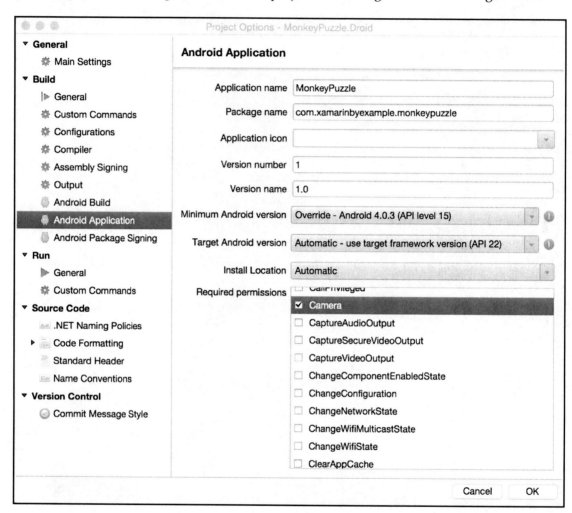

Each application lives in a sandbox in the OS it's installed in. It ensures the end user that an application cannot exit or enter the boundaries of the sandbox. This is a good way to provide security in terms of CPU instructions, memory space, and local storage. If an application needs to communicate with another application (such as contact store, camera, and so on) or device sub-system (such as geoposition, accelerometer, and so on) it should declare it to the OS during installation/first use and the end user should accept this communication.

This is done by Permissions.

Xamarin allows developers to declare required permissions and the end user sees the required permission list during the installation or first use. If the end user does not allow an application to access some of the required permissions, then that application cannot access it.

We will now add a method to our `PuzzleImage` in order to load an image from the camera using XLabs.

To do that, we will use the `TakePicture` method of the `MediaPicker` object:

```
public async Task LoadFromCamera ()
{
    ImageSource = null;
    var mediaPicker = DependencyService.Get<IMediaPicker> ();
    await mediaPicker.TakePhotoAsync (new CameraMediaStorageOptions {
        DefaultCamera = CameraDevice.Front,
        MaxPixelDimension = 400
    }).ContinueWith (t => {
        if (t.IsFaulted) {
            var s = t.Exception.InnerException.ToString ();
        } else if (t.IsCanceled) {
            var canceled = true;
        } else {
            var mediaFile = t.Result;

            Source = ImageSource.FromStream (() => mediaFile.Source);

            return mediaFile;
        }

        return null;
    }, null);
}
```

Now we just need to add the buttons to our UI in order to call these methods and make the feature available for our final users.

Summary

In this chapter, we have developed a simple prototype of a puzzle game using some image processing and the Xamarin.Forms renderers.

We have learned how to take pictures and load images from the gallery.

In the next chapter, we'll create a brand new application targeting all three platforms (Windows, Android, and iOS).

We'll focus on preparing the development environment, creating and developing the project, using Mapthe s SDK, and communicating with the Restful service acting as a web backend.

8

The People Around Me Application

In this chapter we will start to develop a new project, **People Around Me**, with the help of Xamarin.Forms and Web API. We'll start by creating a project on all three platforms (iOS, Android, and Windows Phone). Then, we'll go through the development process and end up with a working solution.

The first thing we'll do is prepare our development machine so it's ready to develop Xamarin.Forms applications. We'll download, install, and set up IDEs and emulators to debug our project.

We'll also develop a service application to act as a web backend. It's important to run some logic on a web backend, as it'll give us the ability to change that logic over time without any end users noticing. It's also good practice to store *important* client-generated data in the web backend.

What is People Around Me doing?

Let's think about the needs first:

- We need an application that finds others around us. Here is the list of requirements we need in our application: the application should provide a page that enables a user to enter their first name and last name, a check-in button, and a Map element.
- When the user opens the application, the Map element displays people with pins via information received from the web backend.

- When the user clicks the button after entering their first name and last name, the application should send the user's info (first name, last name, and geolocation) to the web end.
- Development environment

This time we'll use Windows OS in the development computer and Visual Studio Community Edition as the development IDE.

If we already have Windows installed on our computer, we can skip the Installing Windows 10 section following. If we don't have Windows installed on our computer but have OS X installed, we can easily set up Windows inside of a Mac computer (MacBook, MacBook Pro, MacBook Air, and so on).

Installing Windows 10

The latest version of Windows at the time of writing this book is Windows 10.

We need two things to install Windows 10 onto a Mac: a USB drive with at least 4 GB of space and the Windows 10 ISO.

Of course, we should also back up OS X just in case.

Installing Windows 10 from USB will format the USB drive first, so we should back up any personal files that we don't want to lose.

Downloading Windows 10

In OS X, launch your preferred web browser and navigate to Microsoft's website to download the Windows 10 ISO: `http://www.microsoft.com/software-download/window s1`

As we can see in the following image, there is an edition selection box and a **Confirm** button:

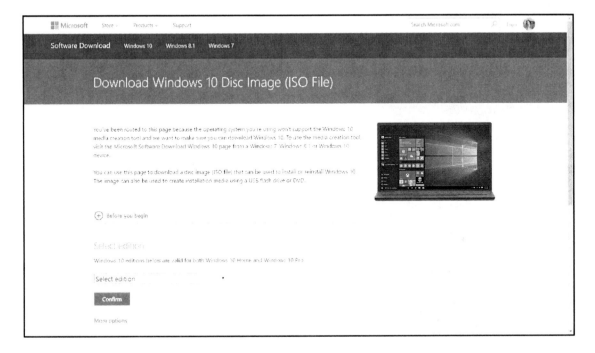

We should select the edition first; here is the list of Windows 10 editions:

- Windows 10
- Windows 10 KN
- Windows 10 N
- Windows 10 Single Language

The Windows 10 N and Windows 10 KN editions are for European and Korean users. These editions don't have media capabilities, so we should skip these editions.

Installing Windows 10 via BootCamp

Once we have downloaded the Windows 10 ISO, we should open up BootCamp on the OS X installed computer. BootCamp comes with every OS X installation and it's free to use. BootCamp walks us through the process, including how to format the USB drive and install ISO files onto it.

BootCamp Assistant will try to connect to Apple's servers to download the latest Windows drivers onto your USB drive. Then, BootCamp Assistant will repartition your hard disk with a Boot Camp partition. Once the partition is configured, our Mac will reboot to continue the Windows installation process.

Installation can take around 15-20 minutes, and the computer will reboot a few times as it installs drivers and configures apps. We have to agree to the usual terms and services before the OS installs.

After installing the OS, we'll see Windows 10's default desktop, as shown in the following image:

After installing and updating Windows 10, we should install Visual Studio 2015. If we already have Visual Studio 2015, we can skip the next section.

Installing Visual Studio 2015

Visual Studio 2015 has a free version, and we can download this free Visual Studio 2015 Community Edition from the Microsoft website (http://www.visualstudio.com). When you log in to the website, you should get the following window:

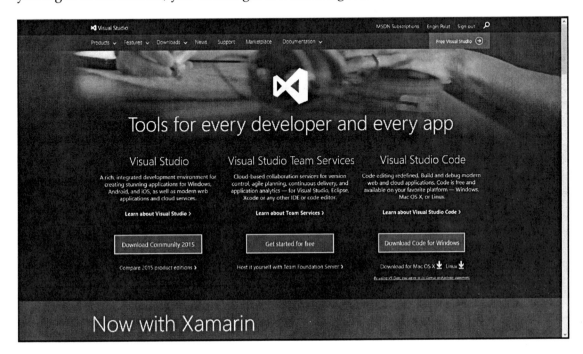

After downloading and installing Visual Studio 2015 Community Edition, we can start to install Xamarin.

If you have already installed Xamarin, you can skip the next section.

Installing Xamarin

To install Xamarin, we have to go to the Xamarin Platforms website (`https://www.xamarin.com/platform`) and download and execute the installer.

Once we have navigated to the Xamarin Platforms web page, there is a button labeled **Download now for free**, as shown in the following image. We can click on it and download the installer.

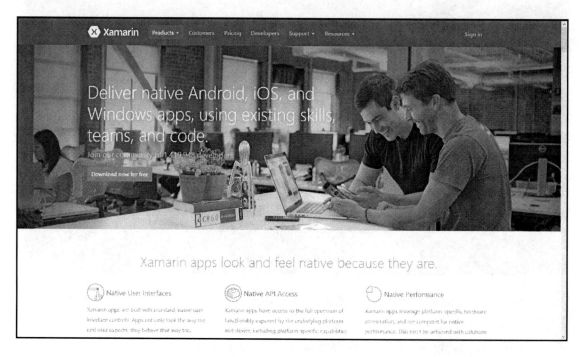

Now we have all we need.

Let's start developing!

Creating the project

First of all, we need to launch Visual Studio 2015. Here is the splash screen of Visual Studio 2015:

After launching Visual Studio 2015, we can create a cross-platform Xamarin project by clicking **File | New Project** and selecting **Cross-Platform** from the left-hand side and selecting **Blank Xaml App (Xamarin.Forms Portable)** from the right-hand side.

Let's name the project `PeopleAroundMe` and click the **OK** button, as shown in the following image:

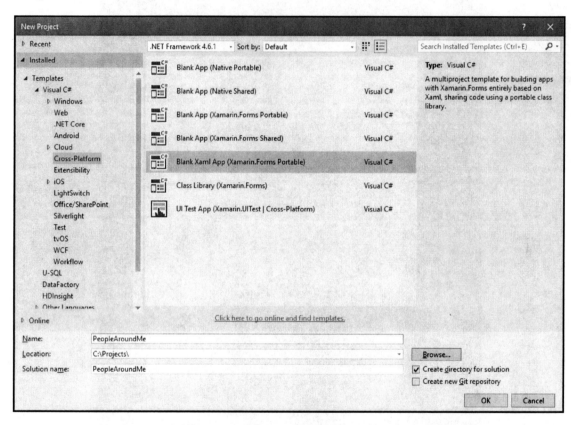

Checking the Android SDK installations

There is an **Open Android SDK Manager** button in the Visual Studio toolbar, and we can click on it and check the installed Android SDKs on our computer.

If the latest Android SDKversions do not exist on our computer, we can easily click the checkboxes and then click on the **Install packagesâ✷** button, as shown in the preceding screenshot.

Check Android virtual devices installation

Microsoft provides great Android emulators, and we can launch an Android emulator from the Visual Studio Emulator for Android application.

If there is no Android Virtual Device installed, we can click on the**Install Profile** button, as shown in the following screenshot:

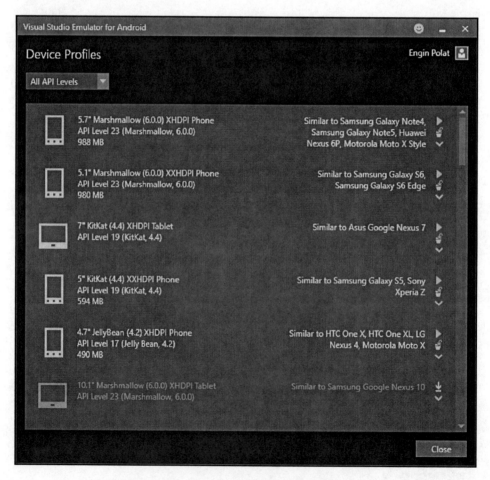

If Android virtual devices are installed on the computer, we can easily start one of them by clicking on the **Launch** button, also shown in the preceding screenshot.

Once the Android virtual device has launched in the emulator, we can use it to debug our application.

There are a few emulators that we can use during the development of our project. Some of them have the ability to fake sensors (such as location, acceleration, camera, and so on), and some of them do not. Some of the emulators are paid applications, and some of them are free. Visual Studio Emulator for Android, for example, has the ability to fake most sensors and it's also free. We can use another emulator during development, of course, but we may also choose to use more than one emulator as well. Here is a list of some of the most common emulators:

Visual Studio Emulator for Android: `http://aka.ms/vscomemudownload`
Android Studio: `http://developer.android.com/studio`
Droid4X: `http://www.droid4x.com`
BlueStacks: `http://www.bluestacks.com`
GenyMotion: `https://www.genymotion.com`
YouWave: `https://youwave.com`

Visual Studio Emulator for Android also has buttons on the right-hand side. They are as follows:

- **Close**
- **Minimize**
- **Power**
- **Single Point Mouse Input**
- **Multi-touch Input**
- **Rotate Left**
- **Rotate Right**
- **Fit to Screen**
- **Zoom**
- **Tools**

When we click on the **Tools** button, a new window appears.

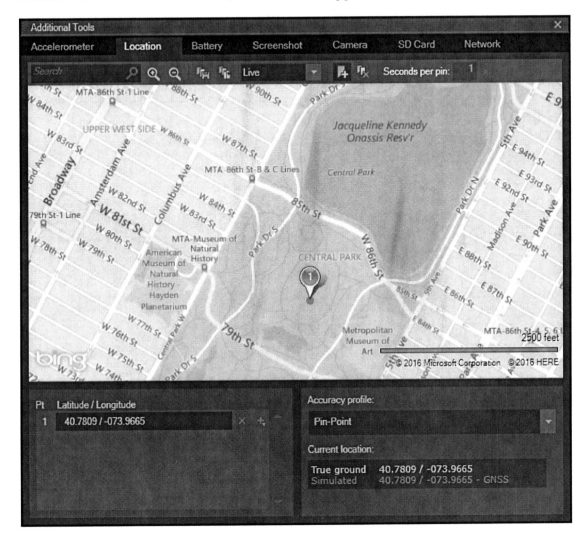

In this new window, we can emulate the following:

- **Accelerometer**
- **GPS coordinates**
- **Camera**
- **SD Card**
- **Network**

Let's leave the Android virtual device running: open up Visual Studio again, right-click on **PeopleAroundMe (Portable)** project, and then click on the **Manage Nuget Packages** menu item.

We should search for the `Xamarin.Forms.Maps` and `Plugin.Geolocator` packages and install them.

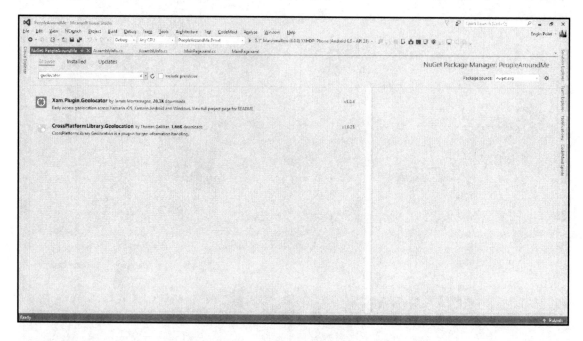

We'll edit the `MainPage.xaml` file from the Visual Studio Solution Explorer panel. We can find it inside the PeopleAroundMe (Portable) project.

There are some xmln (XAML namespace) declarations in the `ContentPage` element. We can think of xmlns as namespace declarations; likewise, our C# namespace declaration.

Now, we're going to compose our `MainPage.xaml` file to display the first name and last name entry fields, the **Add my location to map** button, and the `Map` element.

First of all, we need to add a new xmlns declaration to `ContentPage`:

```
xmlns:maps="clr-namespace:Xamarin.Forms.Maps;assembly=Xamarin.Forms.Maps"
```

Then, we can compose the page as follows:

```
<StackLayout Padding="10" Spacing="10">
    <Label Text="People Around Me" Style="{DynamicResource TitleStyle}" />
    <Entry Placeholder="Enter your first name here" Keyboard="Text"
    x:Name="FirstName" />
    <Entry Placeholder="Enter your last name here" Keyboard="Text"
    x:Name="LastName" />
    <Button Text="Add my location to map" BorderRadius="10"
    Clicked="GetMyLocationAndAddToTheMapButtonClicked"></Button>

    <maps:Map VerticalOptions="FillAndExpand" x:Name="PeopleMap"
    IsShowingUser="true" MapType="Hybrid" />
</StackLayout>
```

We have changed the way the **People Around Me** label looks by setting the `Style` property to `DynamicResource`.

`TitleStyle DynamicResource` changes the element's font to a bigger size.

We have also set the Placeholder properties of the `Entry` elements to explanatory comments.

We can choose a `Map` element's `MapType` property from one of these values:

- Hybrid
- Satellite
- Street (the default)

We can handle the `Button` element's `Clicked` event by adding a method inside Page's `xaml.cs` file. In this example, we'll create a `GetMyLocationAndAddToTheMapButtonClicked` method, as follows:

```
private async void GetMyLocationAndAddToTheMapButtonClicked
(object sender, EventArgs e)
{
    var position = await CrossGeolocator.Current.GetPositionAsync();
}
```

At this point, we need a web backend to handle the server-side behaviors.

We need to add a new project to our solution:

1. Right-click on the solution node on the `Solution Explorer` panel.
2. Click on **Add** | **New Project**.
3. Select **Web** from category list on the left-hand side and **ASP.NET Web Application (.Net Framework)** from the list on the right-hand side.
4. Name the project `PeopleAroundMe.Service`.
5. Click on the **OK** button.

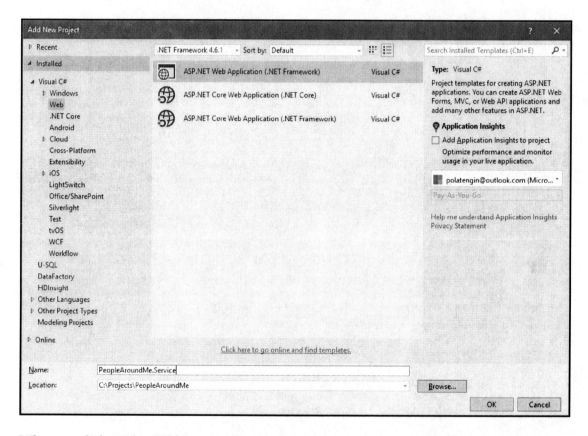

When we click on the **OK** button, a new dialog appears. We have to select a web project template here. The options are as follows, as shown in the following image:

- **Empty**
- **Web Forms**
- **MVC**

- **Web API**
- **Single Page Application**
- **Azure API App**
- **Azure Mobile App**
- **Azure Mobile Service**

We'll select **Empty**, tick the **Web API** checkbox, and develop all the necessary methods.

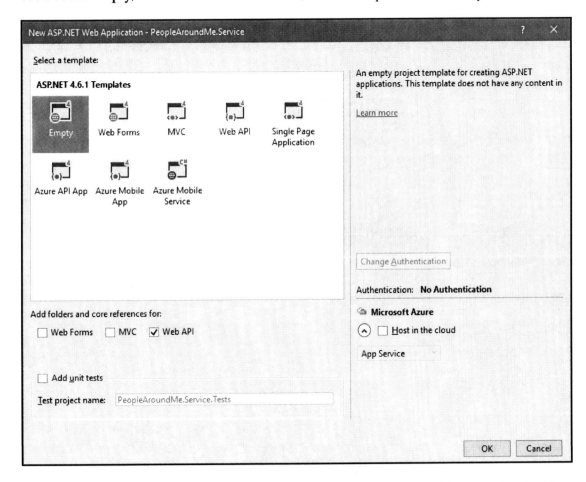

Once the `PeopleAroundMe.Service` project is created, we have to add a new class inside the `Controllers` directory in the `Solution Explorer` panel.

We'll name it `LocationController.cs` and then double-click on the `LocationController.cs` file in **Solution Explorer**.

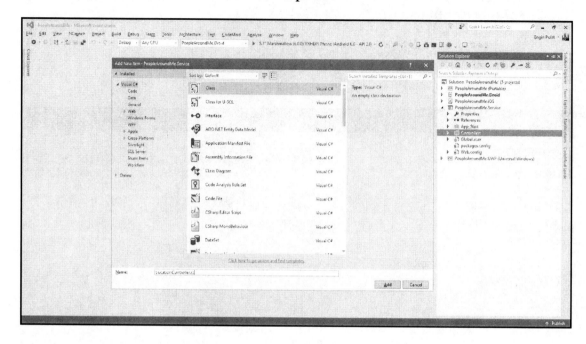

We should change the `LocationController` class' signature and derive it from the `ApiController` base class.

We're going to add a static `List` variable inside of this class to persist the server-side data in memory, and we'll also add two methods to handle `Get` and `Post` requests.

The `Get` method basically returns a static `List` variable.

The `Post` method just adds a new item to that list:

```
public class LocationController : ApiController
{
    private static List<dynamic> peopleData = new List<dynamic>();

    public IEnumerable<dynamic> Get()
    {
        return peopleData;
    }


    public void Post(string fullName, double latitude, double
longitude)
```

```
    {
        peopleData.Add(new { FullName = fullName, Latitude = latitude,
        Longitude = longitude });
    }
}
```

Now we'll open up the `MainPage.xaml.cs` file from the `PeopleAroundMe`
`(Portable)` project and add the following code inside the
`GetMyLocationAndAddToTheMapButtonClicked` method:

```
var param = new FormUrlEncodedContent(new[]
{
  new KeyValuePair<string, string>("fullName",
  FirstName.Text + " " + LastName.Text),
  new KeyValuePair<string, string>("latitude",
  position.Latitude.ToString()),
  new KeyValuePair<string, string>("longitude",
  position.Longitude.ToString())
});

var client = new HttpClient();
var isSuccess = (await client.PostAsync
("http://localhost:XXX/api/location", param)).IsSuccessStatusCode;

if (isSuccess)
{
  var mapPosition = new Position(position.Latitude, position.Longitude);
PeopleMap.MoveToRegion(MapSpan.FromCenterAndRadius(mapPosition,
Distance.FromKilometers(1)));
PeopleMap.Pins.Add(new Pin() { Position = mapPosition, Label = "Me",
Type = PinType.SearchResult });              }
```

Once we start to debug the `PeopleAroundMe.Service` project, the default browser opens
and navigates to `localhost:XXX`, where XXX is a random port number.

Summary

Typically, mobile applications require a web backend. Otherwise, all the data created in the application stays in the device itself. The web backend opens the door from a device into a more common place: the Internet. If the end user removes and installs the application over time, the data may restore. If the end user installs the application on another device, the data may also restore. These are features that accelerate user experience.

In this chapter, we created a web backend and Xamarin.Forms project. The web backend project handles server-side behaviors and the Xamarin.Forms project is working on all three platforms' devices.

During the development phase, we learned how to compose and style Xamarin.Forms pages and how to communicate with the web end.

In the next chapter, we'll test and optimize Xamarin.Forms projects.

9
Testing – Spot the bugs

When we publish any application, it is important that it is *bug free*. This does not mean that *bugs are free* but that the application is carefully designed, developed, and tested so that all the *found* bugs are fixed.

We should take all the required time and effort to find and fix the bugs in the application. To do that, we should profile and test the application continuously and address all the edge cases.

In this chapter, we will explore key features of debugging, profiling, and testing Xamarin.Forms projects.

Debugging a Xamarin project

Debugging is a common part of the development process to remove unexpected behaviours from code files.

Both Xamarin Studio and Visual Studio have great tools to make it easy to detect and fix bugs (the bug is unexpected behaviour itself).

The Xamarin framework is built and run on top of Mono Runtime and implements Mono Soft Debugger. Both IDEs use the Mono Soft Debugger to debug managed code in all Xamarin applications.

Creating a sample project

We'll create a sample project to learn the debugging process of an Xamarin.Forms project.

Let's open up Xamarin Studio and click on the **New Solution** button at the top of the **Solution** Pane, as shown in the following screenshot:

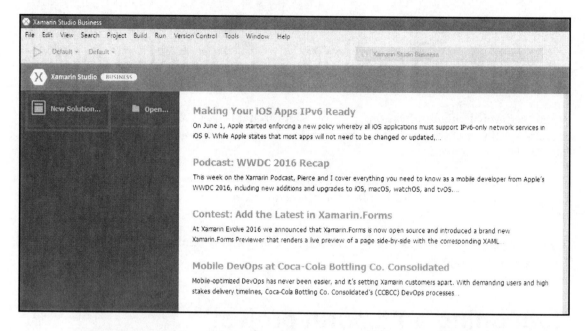

1. Select **Multiplatform** | **App** from the list on the left-hand side, and **Xamarin.Forms** | **Forms App** from the list on the right-hand side.
2. Click on the **Next** button.
3. Type `DebuggingXamarinSample` into the **App Name**.
4. Click on the **Next** button.
5. Review the summary of the project.

6. Click on the **Create** button:

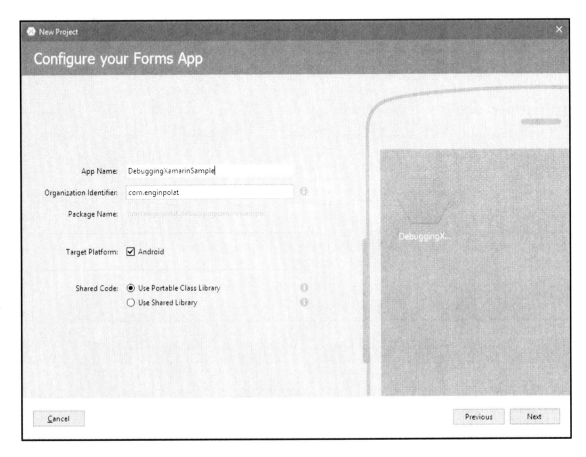

Now we have a new project and we can start to learn the basics of debugging.

Setting a breakpoint

To set a breakpoint, click on the margin area of Xamarin Studio, next to the line number of the code.

The line will turn to a red background and a red circle will appear on the left, as shown in the following screenshot.

When we start the project in **Debug Mode**, the execution will pause on breakpoints:

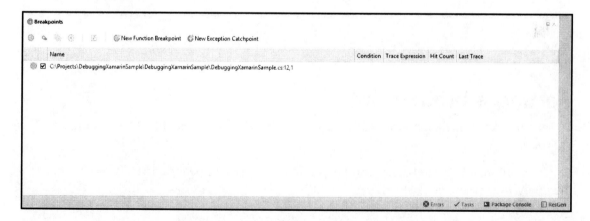

We can view all the breakpoints that have been set in the code file by going to the **Breakpoints Pad**.

If the **Breakpoints Pad** isn't visible, we can make it visible by navigating to **View | Debug Windows | Breakpoints**:

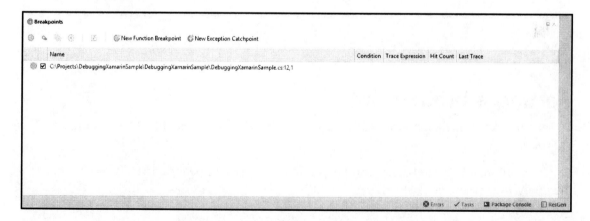

Now that we have breakpoints set, we can easily start a debug session.

Starting a debug session

To start debugging, we need to select the **Debug** option in **Configuration Combo** and click the **Run** button:

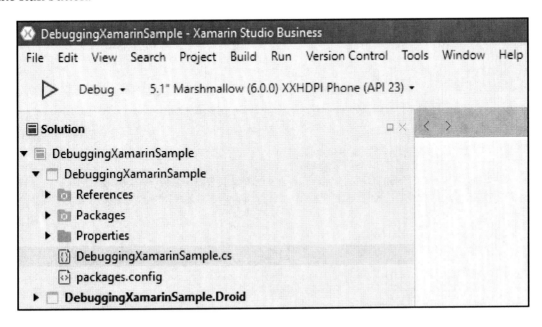

When projects start to run in the emulator and reach the breakpoint, it pauses and gives control to Xamarin Studio.

We can view and change variables' values and control executions step by step, or continue to run at this point.

Usage of log panels

We can use log panels to view execution logs from the running application.

Sometimes we don't want to stop execution and investigate all the variables, or, we can't do that. For example, if there is a loop in a method that iterates hundreds of times and we just want to watch a variables value, we don't want to stop the execution inside the loop.

In this situation, we may use the **Application Output Window Log** panel. Sometimes we want to watch the device's log outputs that our application runs on. In this situation, we may use the **Device Log** panel.

Application output window

When we need to view a variables' values but don't want to pause execution, we can simply use the Log Window of Xamarin Studio.

Simply, we can use the `Console` class' `WriteLine` method and log a variable to the **Application Output** panel:

```
var i = 5;
Console.WriteLine("i is " + i);
```

```
Android Device Log    Application Output      Breakpoints      Locals      Watch      Threads
[Mono] DllImport loaded library '/system/lib/liblog.so'.
[Mono] DllImport searching in: '/system/lib/liblog.so' ('/system/lib/liblog.so').
[Mono] Searching for '__android_log_print'.
[Mono] Probing '__android_log_print'.
[Mono] Found as '__android_log_print'.
i is 5
[Mono] Assembly Ref addref Xamarin.Forms.Platform.Android[0xab084ac0] -> Xamarin.Android.Support.v4[0xab0842e0]: 3
[Mono] DllImport searching in: '__Internal' ('(null)').
[Mono] Searching for 'java_interop_jnienv_call_nonvirtual_object_method_a'.
[Mono] Probing 'java_interop_jnienv_call_nonvirtual_object_method_a'.
[Mono] Found as 'java_interop_jnienv_call_nonvirtual_object_method_a'.
```

Android device log

We can attach to a device and view OS and application level logs in this panel:

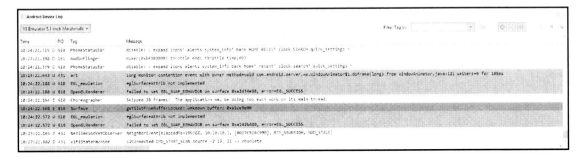

We can even add our own logs to this panel by using the log class and its methods:

- Debug
- Error
- Info
- Warn
- Wtf (What a Terrible Failure)

If we need to add a log on a specific condition, we can write a code like this:

```
var i = 5;
Log.Error("MainWindow", "i = " + i);
```

This code block writes a line inside the **Android Device Log** with a red background, because it's an **Error Log**:

Xamarin Profiler

Profiling in computer programming area is measuring an application's behaviour by collecting values of memory usage, time complexity, CPU usage, and so on. This measurement provides us with a good analysis of the application's usage. With profiling, we can see the overall performance results of an application to a particular method's execution duration.

When we complete an application and submit it to stores, users start to download and use it.

If the application has crashes and errors or bottlenecks, users are likely to abandon it and remove it from their devices.

With this in mind, it's crucial to measure the application's memory, CPU, and network usage to find bottlenecks.

The Xamarin Profiler is a standalone application, and it's integrated with Xamarin Studio and Visual Studio to profile an application.

We need to download and install Xamarin Profiler first; we can find the installer on the Xamarin official website.

Xamarin Profiler provides us a way to profile an Xamarin application from Xamarin Studio or Visual Studio. The Profiler collects and displays information about the app to analyse an application's behavior and usage.

Launching the Profiler

We should launch the Profiler to start collecting data:

1. First, we need to load a solution inside Xamarin Studio.
2. Then, click on the **Run | Start Profiling** menu to open the Profiler.

This launches the Profiler, and automatically starts profiling the application:

We'll select **All Profiles** from the list and click the **Choose** button, as shown in the preceding screenshot.

Now we can use the application normally from the emulator. When we end the application, the Xamarin Profiler stops collecting data.

We can view charts about memory usage, allocated objects in memory, and so on.

We can use these charts to understand the bottlenecks of the application, fix them in code, and run the Profiler again to see the positive difference.

The Xamarin.UITest framework

According to the Xamarin website (`https://developer.xamarin.com/guides/testcloud/uitest/`), Xamarin.UITest is an Automated UI Acceptance Testing framework that allows programmers to write and execute tests in C# and NUnit that validate the functionality of an application.

That means we can write test methods using C# to test the functionality of an Xamarin application. For example, we can test these and many more scenarios:

- Launch the application, wait for the landing page, click on the **SignUp** button, enter **Username, Password, Full Name**, and so on, in the relevant entry fields, click on the **Create** button, and check that the browser naviagates to the Home page
- Launch the application, enter `Mouse` into the search field, click on the **Find** button, wait for the result list to be filled, and check if there are 25 items in the list
- Launch the application, swipe five times to the right, wait for the image to load, click the **Buy** button, and check if the **You have to login first** message appears

Xamarin.UITest uses the Xamarin Test Cloud Agents. Xamarin Test Cloud Agent is an HTTP server that will communicate with the mobile application being tested.

Unfortunately, we can only test Android and iOS applications with the Xamarin.UITest framework. It is not possible to test Windows Phone applications at the time of writing.

Creating a sample UITest project

Let's open Xamarin Studio and create a sample UITest project:

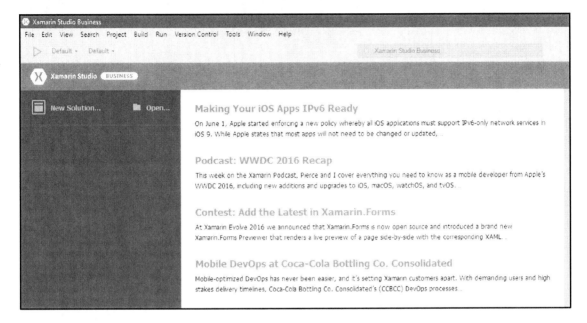

1. Select **Multiplatform | App** from the list on the left-hand side, and **Xamarin.Forms | Forms App** from the list on the right-hand side.
2. Click on the **Next** button.
3. Type UITestSample into the **App Name** field.
4. Click on the **Next** button.
5. Check **Add an automated UI test project** in the **Xamarin Test Cloud** group.

6. Click on the **Create** button:

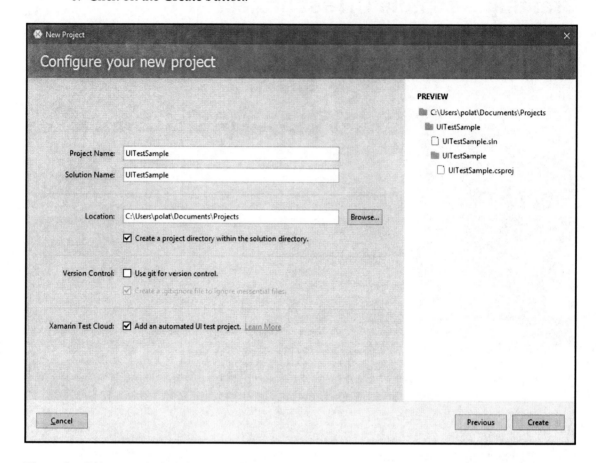

The only difference is that the UITestSample.UITests project was created with solution.

Let's investigate the Test.cs file inside the UITestSample.UITests project by double-clicking on it.

We can see that the Tests class is annotated with a [TestFixture] attribute.

The TestFixture attribute turns the Tests class into a test methods container class.

When testing starts, the TestFixture annotated classes begin to run.

First of all, a method with the [SetUp] attribute annotation is executed. This method handles starting test logic.

Then all the methods with the [Test] attribute annotation are executed.

We should only write the [Test] attribute annotated methods. These methods basically do whatever the client (the application's end user) does with our application by automation:

```
[TestFixture]
public class Tests
{
    AndroidApp app;

    [SetUp]
    public void BeforeEachTest()
    {
        app = ConfigureApp.Android.StartApp();
    }

    [Test]
    public void WelcomeTextIsDisplayed()
    {
        AppResult[] results = app.WaitForElement(c => c.Marked("Welcome
to Xamarin Forms!"));
        app.Screenshot("Welcome screen.");

        Assert.IsTrue(results.Any());
    }
}
```

We can easily see that only the test is waiting for the **Welcome to Xamarin Forms!** label on the screen.

The TextFixture attribute changes classes to test classes. All the methods with a Test attribute listed in the Unit Test Panel can be run to test.

We created a test method to test if the label contains the **Welcome to Xamarin Forms!** text.

The WaitForElement method iteratively queries the parameter to find the matching element. If there is no element that can be found in a timely fashion, TimeoutException will be thrown.

Some of the other methods are listed here:

- ClearText
- EnterText
- Tap
- DoubleTap

- TouchAndHold
- PinchToZoomIn
- PinchToZoomOut
- PressVolumeDown
- PressVolumeUp
- Screenshot
- ScrollDown
- ScrollTo
- ScrollUp
- SetOrientationPortrait
- SetOrientationLandscape
- SwipeRight
- SwipeLeft

We may use these methods to create any test scenario we want using C#. If we use the WaitForElement method, its first parameter is type of AppQuery. The AppQuery class lets us write a query and returns matched view elements.

Some of the methods we may use with AppQuery are listed here:

- All
- Button
- Id
- Index
- Child
- Parent
- TexField
- Marked

These methods take parameters and find the matched view elements.

For example, the All() method returns all view elements in a page.

Another example, the `Marked()` method, takes a parameter and finds its value in all view elements' ID or text fields in page and returns an element if found.

 There is a platform difference here, the `Marked()` method in Android finds an ID, contentDescription, or text fields, in iOS an `accessibilityLabel` or `accessibilityIdentifier` fields.

Assert calls are for what we want to test.

We should open the **Unit Tests** panel by clicking **View** | **Unit Testing** in the Xamarin Studio IDE:

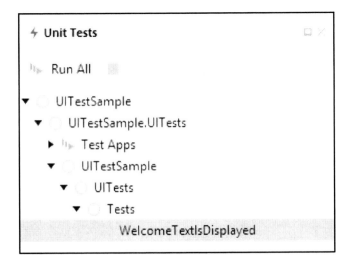

We can run individual tests by right-clicking and clicking **Run** on the menu, or we can run all tests by clicking the **Run All** button.

When tests are completed to run they should be *green*. If there is a *red* test we should check what is wrong and fix it to make the test *green* again:

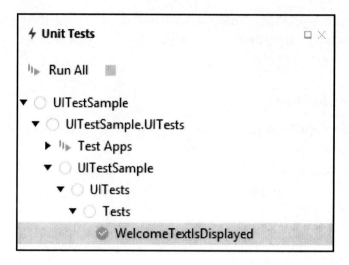

We can easily use the following methods to traverse and interact with the application's UI surface:

- Button
- Id
- Index
- Text
- TextField
- Class
- Marked
- Tap
- Parent
- Query
- PressEnter
- EnterText
- WaitForElement
- Screenshot

With these methods we can easily write thousands of tests to test the application's UI and execute them within seconds.

For example, if we need to test a page with an e-mail address entry box, we may use the following code block:

```
app.WaitForElement(c => c.Marked("lblEmail").Text("Enter
Email")); app.EnterText(c=>c.Marked("txtEmail"),
"test@test"); app.Tap(c => c.Marked("btnSend"));
app.WaitForElement(c =>
c.Marked("lblError").Text("Entered email address is
invalid"));
```

The following list is the test flow: Running test wait for an element appear on the screen, named `lblEmail`, have `Enter Email`
Running test enter `test@test to txtEmail` named element
Running test click on the `btnSend` named element
Running test wait for the `Entered email address is invalid` text appears in the `lblError` named element

Summary

In this chapter, we learnt key features of debugging, profiling, and testing.

We also learned why we should consider profiling our application, testing all the edge cases, and finding hidden bugs all the time. It takes time and effort but it'll be worth it. The more we fix bugs the more end users will like it.

Typically, an application's development process contains several phases, and when it reaches the final phase, starts from the beginning again. Such phases are as follows:

- Analyzing
- Developing
- Testing
- Publishing to store

For example, the first version of the application published to the store, the second version development phases starts from the beginning.

In the next (and final) chapter, we'll investigate mechanisms of publishing to the store.

10
Publishing to the Market

In the mobile world, there are three big OSes, and each OS platform has its own store for applications. In this chapter, we will learn how to publish an application on all three stores in order to reach the maximum user base.

When the App Store launched in 2008, it provided an exciting new way for developers to distribute their apps and games to iPhone users. Since then, stores are the place where end users find applications and games, read reviews about them, view screenshots/watch videos of them in action, and install them to their devices. Each store has their own unique publishing policies and mechanisms. The stores are as follows:

- On iOS, Apple has the App Store
- On Android, Google has the Play Store
- On Windows, Microsoft has the Windows Store

What is store?

When we buy a mobile phone and want to install apps on it, we have to open its store app to find what we want to install and then download it from the app.

Similar to regular stores outside in the real world, stores in platforms give us the opportunity to find and buy things, virtually.

Stores can contain applications, games, albums, movies, and even books, both free and paid.

Free items in stores can easily be downloaded on mobile devices, and paid items must be paid for before they can be downloaded.

Some of the paid items—if the publisher allows it—can be tried inside a trial period.

Each store has its own process for approving or rejecting an application's distribution. There are two types of approvement process: pre-moderation and post-moderation.

Apple and Microsoft use the pre-moderation process, which is where an application needs to be tested and approved *before* it can be findable in the store.

Google, on the other hand, uses the post-moderation process, where an application can be tested and rejected *after* it is findable in the store.

This doesn't mean that the Google store is full of harmful applications, of course. Google will perform some automated tests to detect harmful codes and applications beforehand, but it can't detect badly designed and useless applications.

Apple and Microsoft are more protective in terms of application usability.

A developer may also want to sell an application to a store. All three stores have the ability to sell an application, and they have 70% -30% policy, meaning every transaction (purchase of an application) is split 70%-30%. The developer receives 70% and the store receives 30% as an operating fee.

Microsoft, Google, and Apple are the same, in general, but there are some nuances in terms of payment to developer policies.

In this chapter, we'll investigate how to prepare our application before publishing to stores.

Publishing to the Apple App Store

Once our Xamarin.iOS project development has been completed, the next step is to distribute our application to users.

Apple Developer Portal steps

We should have an Apple Developer Account in order to be able to publish our application to the Apple App Store.

Apple allows us to have Individual or Enterprise Developer Accounts, and one can easily buy either from `https://developer.apple.com`.

As we can see on `https://developer.apple.com/support/compare-memberships`, most of the time, Individual Accounts are enough for publishing applications to the App Store.

> Some of the differences between Individual and Enterprise Developer Accounts are as follows:
>
> Individual Accounts cost $99 per year, distribute applications only via the App Store, and once an application has been built and tested, it should complete the review process before being accepted. The review time typically takes a week.
>
> Enterprise Accounts cost $299 per year and distribute applications via the App Store and sideloading (meaning distributing applications directly to employees). They can receive code-level support. Once an application has been built and tested, it can be launched immediately.

Once we have a Developer Account, we need a Distribution Provisioning Profile to build and publish our application.

The first step is to log in to our Developer Account on the Apple website (`https://developer.apple.com/account`).

After successfully logging in to our account, we can find the Certificates, **Identifiers**, **Devices**, and **Provisioning Profiles** links in the menu on the left.

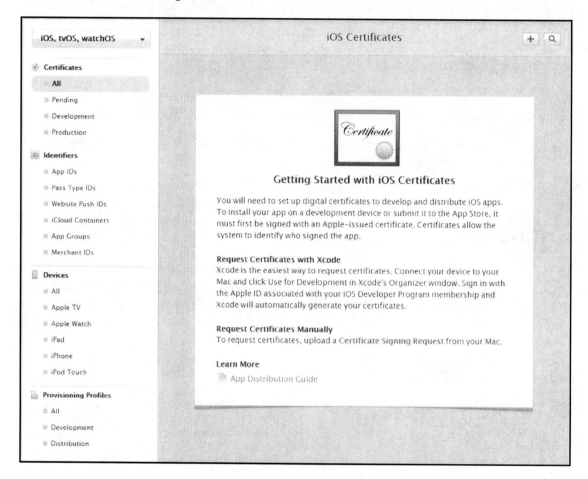

Now, we should click on the **Production** link under the **Certificates** group on the left-hand side menu.

We can click the + button at the top of the content area on the right-hand side.

We should select **App Store and Ad Hoc** and click on the **Continue** button.

Now we should follow the instructions to create a Certificate Signing Request from the Keychain Access application, installed on a Mac computer.

Once we have created our Certificate Signing Request by following the instructions, we can click on the **Continue** button and upload the `.certSigningRequest` file to the Member Center.

Then, we can click on the **Generate** button and the **Download** button to download a certificate, double-clicking on it to install it on our Mac computer.

At this point, we should see our certificate in Xcode.

We now have a Distribution Certificate, so we need to register an App ID in order to distribute our app to the App Store.

We can click on **App IDs** under **Identifiers** from the left-hand side menu.

We should click on the + button to add a new App ID, providing a name.

Then, click on the **Continue** button and complete the process as instructed on screen.

Now that we have the Distribution Certificate and App ID, we need to compile a Distribution Profile and publish our project via the App Store.

We can click on **Distribution** under **Provisioning Profiles** from the left-hand side menu.

We can click on the + button at the top of the content area on the right-hand side menu.

We should choose the App Store option under the **Distribution** category.

Click on the **Continue** button and select the App ID that we just created from the list.

Click on the **Continue** button a couple more times and then click on the **Generate** button at the end of the steps to finalize the process.

Visual Studio steps

When we are ready to compile our application to upload it to the App Store, we'll need to select the Distribution Profile that we just created.

Let's right-click on the iOS project in **Solution Explorer** and select the **Properties** menu.

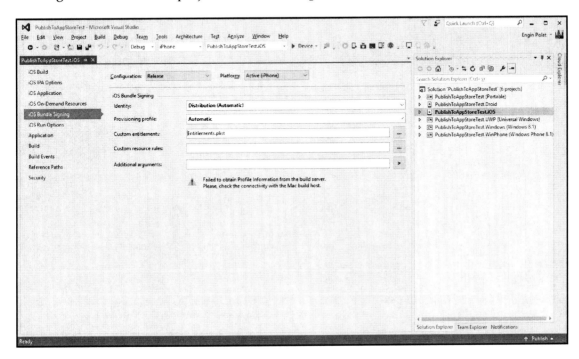

Click on the **iOS Bundle Signing** menu on the left-hand side menu and change the **Configuration** to **Release** and **Platform** to **Active (iPhone).**

Change Identity to **Distribution (Automatic)** and **Provisioning Profile** to **Automatic.**

Save the **Properties** window.

After compiling our project, there will be a `*.IPA` file in our project directory; we need to log in to the iTunes Connect website at `http://itunesconnect.apple.com` to upload it.

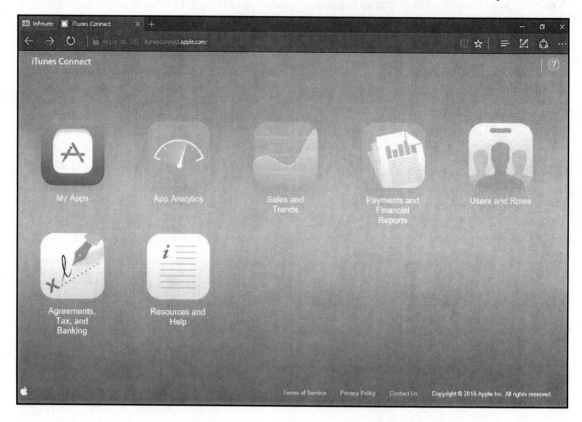

Once we have logged in to iTunes Connect, we can register the app using the **My Apps** link.

We'll follow the instructions on the page and register our app to iTunes Connect.

There is one more step, which is to upload the compiled binaries to the iTunes Connect site.

Now we have to wait for our application to go through the approval process, and after it's approved, it will appear on the Apple App Store.

Publishing to the Google Play Store

Publishing is a two-step process, and it starts with compilation of a `Xamarin.Android` project and ends with uploading a compiled package to the store.

We need a Google Developer Account in order to upload our package to the Google Play Store.

Preparing Project to Compile

It's strongly recommended that applications have their unique icons. In Visual Studio, we can assign an application icon using the **Android Manifest** section of project **Properties**, as shown in the following screenshot:

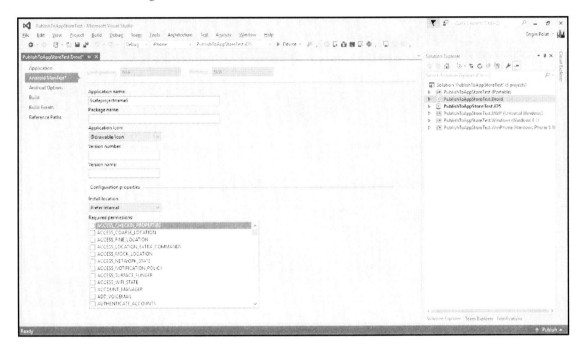

We also have to specify the **Version number** and **Version name** of the application, as shown in the preceding screenshot.

The `AssemblyInfo.cs` file can contain the assembly: Application attribute, so we should compile our project as non-debuggable by adding `[assembly: Application(Debuggable=false)]` to the `AssemblyInfo.cs` file.

Debuggable compiled applications require extra steps when running to announce their state and extra information to the debugger, which generally results in poor performance.

Creating a package

Since Xamarin.Android 4.2.6, we have the **Publish Android Application** menu item under the **Tools** menu of Visual Studio.

The **Publish Android Application** menu helps us to create an APK package of our project.

> If the **Publish Android Application** menu is disabled, we have to make sure that the project configuration is set to **Release** debugging is disabled, and make sure the project is selected in the **Solution Explorer**.

We need to specify the **Location** and **Password** to create a KeyStore, which we'll use to sign our project and generate an APK package, as shown in the following screenshot:

After clicking on the **Next** button, we'll fill in the form with the information shown in the following screenshot:

We'll click on the **Next** button again and check the location and name of the soon-to-be created APK package file, as shown in the following screenshot:

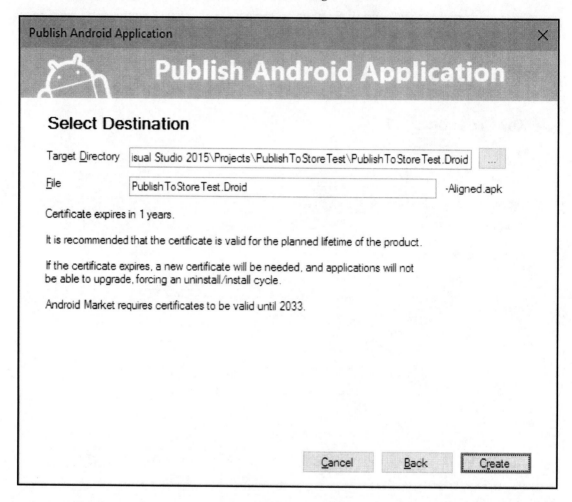

When the **Create** button is clicked, Visual Studio compiles and signs the project and creates an APK package file.

Publishing an application on the Google Play Store

There are several Android application stores out there, for example, the Amazon AppStore for Android, but the Google Play Store is indeed the largest and most visited store in the world for Android applications.

First of all, we need to have a publisher account in order to publish our application. We can get one from the Google Play Developer Console (`https://play.google.com/apps/publish`) page by entering basic information and paying a $25 registration fee.

Once we have created a publisher account, we can log in to the Google Play Developer Console and publish an application by clicking on the **Publish an Android App on Google Play** button, as follows:

After clicking on the **Publish an Android App on Google Play** button, a popup is shown inviting us to enter the **Title** of our application and upload the APK package file, as follows:

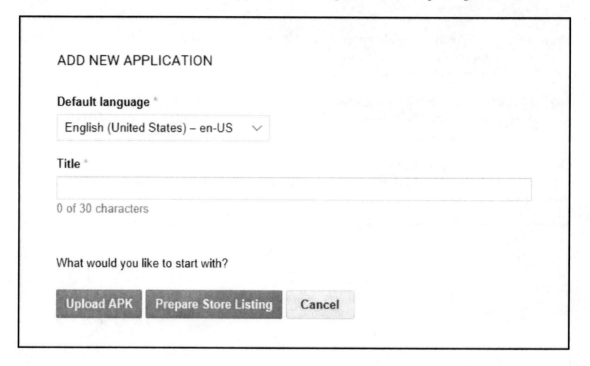

After uploading the APK package file, we should also upload some screenshots of our application's pages. Enter a description and any recent changes (if applicable) and select the application type and category.

We should follow the instructions on screen and complete the publishing process.

In a few minutes (less than an hour usually), our application should show up on the Google Play Store and users will be able to find and install it onto their devices.

Some of the edge cases cause Google Play Store to reject our application without enabling it to be found. For example, Age Ratings, Encryption, and so on may cause our app to be rejected.

Publishing to the Windows Store

The third store we need to publish our application on is Microsoft's Windows Store.

The steps for publishing our application to the Windows Store are not so different to the other stores' publishing steps.

We need a Windows Developer Account and can easily obtain one from the `https://devel oper.microsoft.com/registration` page. We should follow the instructions on the page and pay a one-off fee of $19 to get a developer account. This is the cheapest price for a developer account on all app stores.

After creating a Windows Developer Account, we should go to Visual Studio and focus on the **UWP (Universal Windows Platform)** project in our solution; we can find it in the **Solution Explorer** panel.

We'll right-click on the UWP project and click on the **Store | Associate** app with the **Store** menu.

A new window appears and lets us update one of our previously-created applications or create a new application, as shown in the following screenshot:

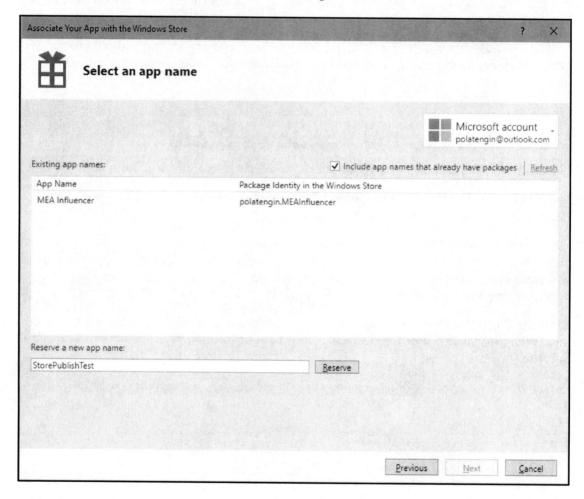

After selecting an existing application or entering a new name and clicking on the **Reserve** button, we have to click on the **Next** button.

A new window displays the information about our application to us, as follows:

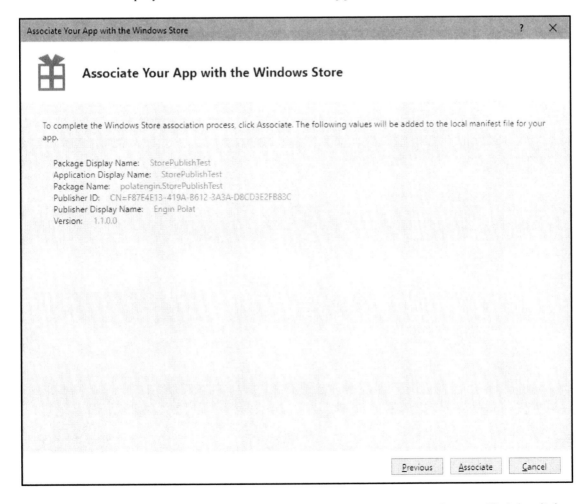

Finally, we need to click the Associate button to finalize the process. Now, we'll right-click on the UWP or Windows project and select the **Store** | **Create App Packages** menu item.

A new window will pop up and let us choose to either create package for the Windows Store or side-loading, as follows:

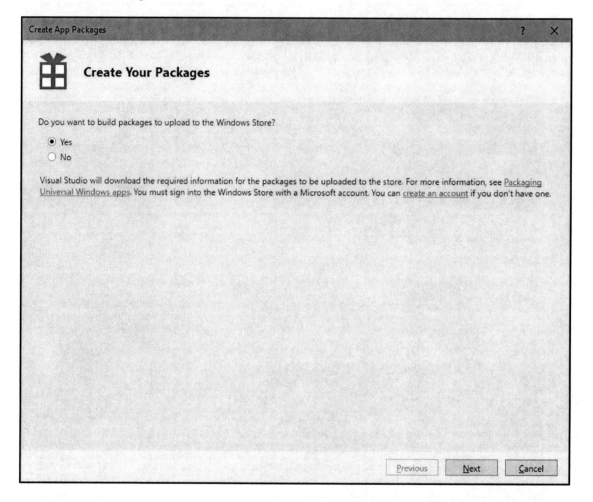

 Created packages can be uploaded to the Windows Store to be found by end users and installed on a device. Side-loading is another way to install an application to a device, and it's done by pushing the package to the device and forcing Windows to install it. This way is more suitable if you want to install an application to all of your enterprise's employees.

We'll continue with the **Yes** option selected and then click on the **Next** button. A new page lets us select an output directory, the version of the application, and supported CPU architectures.

 We can use language-specific resources, lots of different scaled images, and different CPU architectures. AppBundle contains bits for specific languages, specific display scales, and specific CPU architectures. The application will run in the same way but it will take up less space and users will need to download and store less for the same application.

We'll enter the required information in this page and click on the **Create** button to create the application packages, as shown in the following screenshot:

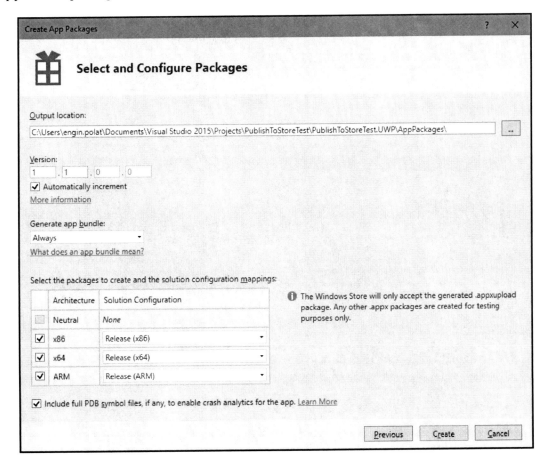

Now we can go to the `https://developer.microsoft.com/dashboard/apps/overview` page and click on an application name in the Application List.

We can start publishing our application by clicking on the **Start your submission** button, as follows:

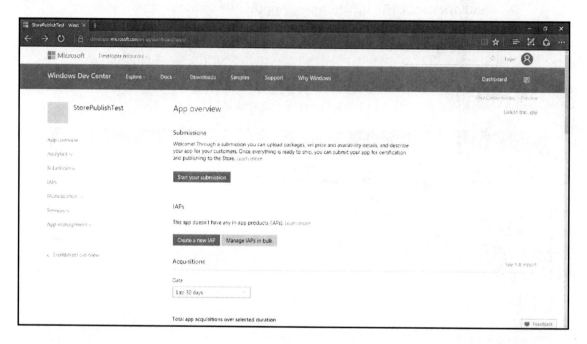

First of all, we need to select pricing for our application. We can always choose **Free**, choose a price from the list, or let users have a free trial period.

We can select our application to be in the store as soon as it passes certification or on a specific date.

We can select our application's category and sub-category from the list.

We can select hardware support required from end users in order to install our application to their devices, for example, NFC, Bluetooth, mouse, and so on.

The next step is the age rating, and we should answer the questionnaire's options following the instructions on screen.

Then, we should upload the required packages to store by dragging and dropping them on the screen.

After uploading the packages, we can upload screenshots and app icons as well. We can also provide a descriptive summary of our application.

Microsoft testers should test our application and certify it to be available on the Windows Store. If our application needs login credentials or requires anything to be tested, we can provide them via the **Notes for certification** step.

After all the steps are completed, we can click on the *Submit to the Store* button and wait for the certification.

Microsoft testers will test our application and will certify our application to be shown in the Store as soon as possibly—if everything goes well, of course.

Summary

During the course of this book, we prepared our development machine; learned about different view elements, layouts, and page types by using them; communicated with the web backend with different techniques, and last but not least we learned how to profile, debug, and test our project, and fine-tune it to be ready to publish.
In this final chapter, we learned all the different stores of the different platforms we can publish our application to and we walked step by step to upload our application to all these stores. Now we can build and publish as many applications as we want, and cheer the love of users to our applications.
From here, we can follow the road and learn about In App Purchases, Push Notifications, Analytics, Ad Mediation, UX Patterns and some services provided by Microsoft, Google, and Apple.

Index

CPSIA information can be obtained
at www.ICGtesting.com
Printed in the USA
FFOW04n2227261217
44178892-43592FF